Further praise for

MORE THAN JUST RACE

"A refreshing, multilayered study of racial inequality in America."
—*Kirkus Reviews*

"[Wilson] makes a bold effort to reframe current debates on the relationship between poverty and race in the U.S. . . . [He] combines a critical look at recent research on poverty and race with his own field research to construct a synthesis that sidesteps many of the pitfalls that often entrap race and poverty theorists." —*Publishers Weekly*

"Over the past 30 years, the legendary Harvard sociologist has done more than any other social scientist to illuminate the desperate plight of the poor. . . . *More Than Just Race* contains an important and hopeful shift in Wilson's thinking about how Americans can be persuaded to rally behind a new war on ghetto poverty." —Jack White, *The Root*

"For decades William Julius Wilson has shined a penetrating light on the daunting obstacles that confront the inner-city black poor. In *More Than Just Race* he brilliantly deepens his careful, incisive, unflinching exploration of this subject. Especially in this season of new political possibilities, Wilson's illuminating analysis is a must-read."
—Randall Kennedy, author of *Race and the Law* and
Nigger: The Strange Career of a Troublesome Word

"This book is vintage Wilson: cogent, controversial, and consequential. *More Than Just Race* offers a meticulous review and critical appraisal of the respective roles of social structure and culture in the plight of inner-city blacks. It will excite scholars, policy makers, and citizens eager to think their way through the maze of race, class, and poverty in America."
—Loïc Wacquant, author of *Urban Outcasts* and *Punishing the Poor*

"*More Than Just Race* stands as the next essential chapter in William Julius Wilson's careful ruminations on race and class, equality and opportunity in American life. With dispassion and reason, Wilson grapples with the endless cultural arguments that pit individual responsibility and culture against institutional forces as explanations for persistent urban poverty. By acknowledging both the cultural and institutional forces and moving briskly forward, Wilson leads us to an inevitable political moment: A new war on poverty must be fought, with strategies that acknowledge the arguments of conservatives and liberals alike. But fight we must."
—David Simon, creator, HBO's *The Wire*

"In a forceful repudiation of the conventions of colorblindness, Wilson calls upon social scientists and policy makers to confront the problem of durable inequality anew. Wilson argues that deep-in-the-bone racial indifference, seemingly neutral policies like highway construction, and the weakening of informal job information networks all work together to reinforce the architecture of racial isolation. In order to intervene constructively, policy makers need to galvanize *political will*. But first they need the *intellectual will* to probe beyond conventional wisdom on either the right or the left to explore the structural foundations and the cultural adaptations that cement the linkage between being black and poor in the inner city."
—Lani Guinier, Bennett Boskey Professor of Law, Harvard University

"William Julius Wilson is one of the nation's foremost thinkers and advocates for poor Americans. At this moment in our history, Bill's voice and ideas are needed more than ever. In *More Than Just Race*, Bill tackles some of the toughest and most intractable issues facing our country in a hopeful and powerful way. The intersection of race and poverty in America needs the kind of head-on, incisive treatment that is Bill's trademark." —Angela Glover Blackwell, founder/CEO, PolicyLink

"Wilson has given us a compellingly evidence-based comparison of the socioeconomic and cultural causes of African American urban poverty and its consequences. His insightful analysis enables us to confront the continuing moral and political question: how to allocate the blame and the responsibility for the worsening plight and pathology among so many of the country's poorest citizens."

—Herbert J. Gans, author of *Imagining America in 2033*

"A courageous, provocative, and penetrating analysis that powerfully illuminates the true social condition of the urban poor—essential reading for anyone interested in urban inequality in America."

—Elijah Anderson, Yale University

Also by William Julius Wilson

There Goes the Neighborhood (coauthor)
Good Kids from Bad Neighborhoods (coauthor)
The Bridge over the Racial Divide
When Work Disappears
The Truly Disadvantaged
The Declining Significance of Race
Power, Racism, and Privilege
American Becoming (coeditor)
Poverty, Inequality and the Future of Social Policy (coeditor)
Sociology and the Public Agenda (editor)
The Ghetto Underclass (editor)
Through Different Eyes (coeditor)

Issues of Our Time

Ours has been called an information age, but, though information has never been more plentiful, ideas are what shape and reshape our world. "Issues of Our Time" is a series of books in which some of today's leading thinkers explore ideas that matter in the new millennium. The authors—including the philosopher Kwame Anthony Appiah, the sociologist William Julius Wilson, the social psychologist Claude Steele, legal scholars Charles Fried and Alan Dershowitz, the Pulitzer Prize–winning critic Louis Menand, and the Nobel Prize–winning economist Amartya Sen—honor clarity without shying away from complexity; these books are both genuinely engaged and genuinely engaging. Each recognizes the importance not just of our values but also of the way we resolve the conflicts among those values. Law, justice, identity, morality, and freedom: concepts such as these are at once abstract and utterly close to home. Our understanding of them helps define who we are and who we hope to be; we are made by what we make of them. These are books, accordingly, that invite the reader to reexamine hand-me-down assumptions and to grapple with powerful trends. Whether you are moved to reason together with these authors, or to argue with them, they are sure to leave your views tested, if not changed. The perspectives of the authors in this series are diverse, the voices are distinctive, the issues are vital.

HENRY LOUIS GATES JR., SERIES EDITOR

W. E. B. DU BOIS PROFESSOR OF THE HUMANITIES

HARVARD UNIVERSITY

Issues of Our Time

Other titles

KWAME ANTHONY APPIAH
Cosmopolitanism

AMARTYA SEN
Identity and Violence: The Illusion of Destiny

ALAN DERSHOWITZ
Preemption: A Knife That Cuts Both Ways

CHARLES FRIED
Modern Liberty and the Limits of Government

LOUIS MENAND
The Marketplace of Ideas: Reform and Resistance in the American University

CLAUDE STEELE
Whistling Vivaldi and Other Clues to How Stereotypes Affect Us

Forthcoming authors

AMY GUTMANN
NICHOLAS LEMANN

MORE THAN JUST RACE

BEING BLACK AND POOR IN THE INNER CITY

William Julius Wilson

W. W. NORTON & COMPANY
NEW YORK • LONDON

For information about permission to reproduce selections from this book,
write to Permissions, W. W. Norton & Company, Inc., 500 Fifth Avenue,
New York, NY 10110

For information about special discounts for bulk purchases, please contact
W. W. Norton Special Sales at specialsales@wwnorton.com or 800-233-4830

Manufacturing by Courier Westford
Production manager: Anna Oler

Library of Congress Cataloging-in-Publication Data

Wilson, William J., 1935–
More than just race : being black and poor in the inner city /
William Julius Wilson.
p. cm.
Includes bibliographical references and index.
ISBN 978-0-393-06705-7 (hardcover)
1. Equality—United States. 2. African-Americans—Social conditions.
3. Social classes—United States. 4. Inner cities—United States. I. Title.
HM821.W55 2009
305.5'690899607301732—dc22   2008051239

ISBN 978-0-393-33763-1 pbk.

W. W. Norton & Company, Inc.
500 Fifth Avenue, New York, N.Y. 10110
www.wwnorton.com

W. W. Norton & Company Ltd.
Castle House, 75/76 Wells Street, London W1T 3QT

7 8 9 0

To Jittima

CONTENTS

ACKNOWLEDGMENTS

In the preparation of this book, I am indebted to a number of individuals. I am grateful to my editors at W. W. Norton—Roby Harrington and Mollie Eisenberg—for helpful comments on various drafts that improved the clarity of my arguments and the overall flow of the manuscript. I owe a great deal to Susan Allan for her assistance in making the book more accessible to a lay audience, to Edward Walker for his careful proofreading and editing of various drafts of the manuscript, and to Stephanie Hiebert for skillful copyediting that further improved the book's readability. I would also like to thank Anmol Chaddha for his careful research of library materials and government documents used in *More than Just Race*.

I am also indebted to the following scholars, who read an entire draft of the manuscript and provided detailed and insightful comments that led to significant revisions: Deirdre Bloome, Anmol Chaddha, Michèle Lamont, Christopher Muller, James Quane, Eva Rosen, Tommie Shelby, and Van Tran. Furthermore, I am grateful for the exchange of ideas I had with Robert Asen, Mario Small, and Erik Olin Wright that are reflected in a number of arguments in the book.

Finally, I would like to give a very special thanks to Jessica Houston Su, the coordinator of the Joblessness and Urban Poverty Program that I direct at Harvard University. She improved various drafts of the manuscript with her substantive and editorial comments; and her creative synthesis of materials from a number of archival documents, government documents, and secondary literature greatly facilitated not only my analysis of data, but the organization of my arguments as well.

All of the chapters in this book are original, although a few rewritten paragraphs and quotations from my book *When Work Disappears* (copyright © 1996 by William Julius Wilson and used by permission of Alfred A. Knopf, a division of Random House) are integrated into Chapters 3 and 4. And parts of an essay I wrote, entitled "The Economic Plight of Inner-City Black Males" (from *Against the Wall: Poor, Young, Black, and Male*, edited by Elijah Anderson, copyright © 2008, used by permission of University of Pennsylvania Press) were integrated into Chapter 3.

CHAPTER 1

STRUCTURAL AND CULTURAL FORCES THAT CONTRIBUTE TO RACIAL INEQUALITY

I am an internationally known Harvard professor, yet a number of unforgettable experiences remind me that, as a black male in America looking considerably younger than my age, I am also feared. For example, several times over the years I have stepped into the elevator of my condominium dressed in casual clothes and could immediately tell from the body language of the other residents in the elevator that I made them feel uncomfortable. Were they thinking, "What is this black man doing in this expensive condominium? Are we in any danger?" I once sarcastically said to a nervous elderly couple who hesitated to exit the elevator because we were all getting off on the same floor, "Not to worry, I am a Harvard professor and I have lived in this building for nine years." When I am dressed casually, I am always a little relieved to step into an empty elevator, but I am not apprehensive if I am wearing a tie.

I get angry each time I have an experience like the encounter in the elevator. It would be easy to say that the residents' reaction to me is simply another manifestation of racism. However, when I lived in a middle-class Chicago neighborhood that bordered a ghetto neighborhood, I, too, would tense up when I walked my dog at night and saw a black man or a group of black male teenagers approaching me on the street. The portrayal of black men in the media and their widely known disproportionate rates of incarceration may have influenced some of the residents in my condominium when they saw me in casual clothes. This experience is exacerbated for low-skilled black males and, as we shall see in Chapter 3, is especially problematic when employers assess the suitability of black males for jobs. This is a cultural phenomenon in which people respond to perceptions about black men depicted in the electronic and print media, including racist perceptions. But as a sociologist, from years of research and study I am also aware of and understand the structural reasons—including the limited availability of economic and social opportunities—for the extremely high crime rates of young black men from ghetto neighborhoods. Indeed, I will spend some time discussing the plight of black males in Chapter 3, basing the current exploration on this previous scholarship.

Although we have made considerable progress since the days of Jim Crow segregation, it is clear that we still have a long way to go. Indeed, one of the legacies of historic racial subjugation in this country is the extremely high crime rate among black males, including the violent crime rate. And as long as these disturbing rates persist, people of all racial and ethnic groups will often react to black males in public and private spaces in negative ways.

These problems will not be addressed, however, if we are not willing to have an honest and open discussion of race in America, including a discussion of why poverty and unequal opportunity so stubbornly persist in the lives of so many African Americans. We depend on the work of social scientists to help us come to grips with and understand these issues. However, social scientists have yet to find common ground on how to explain the social and economic destinies of African Americans.

In *More than Just Race* I hope to further our understanding of the complex and interrelated factors that continue to contribute to racial inequality in the United States. In the process, I call for reexamining the way social scientists discuss two important factors associated with racial inequality: *social structure* and *culture*. Although the book highlights the experiences of inner-city African Americans, the complexities of understanding race and racial inequality in America are not limited to research on blacks. Formal and informal aspects of inequality have also victimized Latinos, Asian Americans, and Native Americans. In this book, however, I use the research on inner-city African Americans to elaborate my analytic framework because they have been the central focus of the structure-versus-culture dispute.

This book will likely generate controversy because I dare to take culture seriously as one of the explanatory variables in the study of race and urban poverty—a topic that is typically considered off-limits in academic discourse because of a fear that such analysis can be construed as "blaming the victim." Nonetheless, I hope I can convince the reader of the urgent need for a more frank and honest discussion of complex factors that create and reinforce racial inequality and to rethink the way we talk about addressing the problems of race and urban poverty in the public policy arena.

We should be clear about what we mean by these two important concepts: social structure and culture. *Social structure* refers to the way social positions, social roles, and networks of social relationships are arranged in our institutions, such as the economy, polity, education, and organization of the family. A social structure could be a labor market that offers financial incentives and threatens financial punishments to compel individuals to work; or it could be a "role," associated with a particular social position in an organization such as a church, family, or university (e.g., pastor, head of a household, or professor), that carries certain power, privilege, and influence external to the individuals who occupy that role.[1]

Culture, on the other hand, refers to the sharing of outlooks and modes of behavior among individuals who face similar place-based circumstances (such as poor segregated neighborhoods) or have the same social networks (as when members of particular racial or ethnic groups share a particular way of understanding social life and cultural scripts that guide their behavior). Therefore, when individuals act according to their culture, they are following inclinations developed from their exposure to the particular traditions, practices, and beliefs among those who live and interact in the same physical and social environment.[2]

In this book I try to demonstrate the importance of understanding not only the independent contributions of social structure and culture, but also how they interact to shape different group outcomes that embody racial inequality. When we talk about the impact of structure or culture, we are making explicit references to the forces they set in motion that affect human behavior. To help set up this analysis, let's take a close look at these structural and cultural forces.

Understanding the Impact of Structural Forces

Two types of structural forces contribute directly to racial group outcomes such as differences in poverty and employment rate: social acts and social processes. *Social acts* refers to the behavior of individuals within society. Examples of social acts are stereotyping; stigmatization; discrimination in hiring, job promotions, housing, and admission to educational institutions—as well as exclusion from unions, employers' associations, and clubs—when any of these are the act of an individual or group exercising power over others.

Social processes refers to the "machinery" of society that exists to promote ongoing relations among members of the larger group. Examples of social processes that contribute directly to racial group outcomes include laws, policies, and institutional practices that exclude people on the basis of race or ethnicity. These range from explicit arrangements such as Jim Crow segregation laws and voting restrictions to more subtle institutional processes, such as school tracking that purports to be academic but often reproduces traditional segregation, racial profiling by police that purports to be about public safety but focuses solely on minorities, and redlining by banks that purports to be about sound fiscal policy but results in the exclusion of blacks from home ownership. In all of these cases, ideologies about group differences are embedded in organizational arrangements.

Many social observers who are sensitive to and often outraged by the direct forces of racism, such as discrimination and segregation, have paid far less attention to those political and economic forces that *indirectly* contribute to racial inequality.[3] I have in mind political actions that have an impact on racial group outcomes, even though they are not explicitly designed or publicly discussed as matters involving race, as well as impersonal economic forces that reinforce long-standing forms of racial inequality. These structural forces are classified as indirect because they are mediated by the racial groups' position in the system of social stratification (the extent to which the members of a group occupy positions of power, influence, privilege, and prestige). In other words, economic changes and political decisions may have a greater adverse impact on some groups than on others simply because the former are more vulnerable as a consequence of their position in the social stratification system. These indirect structural forces are often so massive in their impact on the social position and experiences of people of color that they deserve full consideration in any attempt to understand the factors leading to differential outcomes along racial lines.

Take, for instance, impersonal economic forces, which sharply increased joblessness and declining real wages among many poor African Americans in the last several decades. As with all other Americans, the economic fate of African Americans is inextricably connected with the structure and functioning of a much broader, globally influenced modern economy. In recent years, the growth and spread of new technologies and the growing internationalization of economic activity have changed the relative demand for different types of workers. The wedding of emerging technologies and international competition has eroded the basic institutions of the mass production system and eradicated related manufacturing jobs in the United States. In the last several decades, almost all of the improvements in productivity have been associated with technology and human capital, thereby drastically reducing the importance of physical capital and natural resources. The changes in technology that are producing new jobs are making many others obsolete.

Although these trends tend to benefit highly educated or highly skilled workers, they have contributed to the growing threat of job displacement and eroding wages for unskilled workers. This development is particularly problematic for African Americans, who have a much higher proportion of workers in low-skilled jobs than whites have. As the late black economist Vivian Henderson argued three decades ago, racism put blacks in their economic place, but changes in the modern economy make the place in which they find themselves more and more precarious.[4]

The workplace has been revolutionized by technological changes that range from mechanical development like robotics to advances in information technology like computers and the Internet. While even educated workers are struggling to keep pace with technological changes, lower-skilled workers with less education are falling behind with the increased use of information-based technologies and computers, and they face the growing threat of job displacement in certain industries.[5] To illustrate, in 1962 the employment-to-population ratio—the percentage of adults who are employed—was 52.5 percent for those with less than a high school diploma, but by 1990 it had plummeted to 37.0 percent. By 2006 it had rebounded slightly, to 43.2 percent, possibly because of the influx of low-skilled Latino immigrants in low-wage service sector jobs.[6]

In the new global economy, highly educated, well-trained men and women are in demand, as illustrated most dramatically by the sharp differences in employment experiences among men. Compared to men with lower levels of education, college-educated men spend more time working, not less.[7] The shift in the demand for labor is especially devastating for low-skilled workers whose incorporation into the mainstream economy is marginal or recent. Even before the economic restructuring of the nation's economy, low-skilled African Americans were at the end of the employment line, often the last to be hired and the first to be let go.

The computer revolution is a major reason for the shift in the demand for skilled workers. Even "unskilled" jobs such as fast-food service require employees to work with computerized systems, even though they are not considered skilled workers. Whereas only one-quarter of US workers directly used a computer on their jobs in 1984, by 2003 that figure had risen to more than half (56.1 percent) of the workforce.[8] According to the economist Alan Krueger, "The expansion of computer use can account for one-third to two-thirds of the increase in the payoff of education between 1984 and 1993 [in the United States]."[9] Krueger gives two reasons for this expansion: First, even after a number of background factors such as experience and education are taken into account, those who use computers at work tend to be paid more than those who do not. Second, the industries with the greatest shift in employment toward more highly skilled workers are those in which computer technology is more intensively used.

The shift in the United States away from low-skilled workers can also be related to the growing internationalization of economic activity, including increased trade with countries that have large numbers of low-skilled, low-wage workers.[10] Two developments facilitated the growth in global economic activity: (1) advances in information and communication technologies, which enabled companies to shift work to areas around the world where wages for unskilled work are much lower than in the "first world"; and (2) the expansion of free trade, which reduced the price of imports and raised the output of export industries. But increases in imports that compete with labor-intensive industries (e.g., apparel, textile, toys, footwear, and some manufacturing) hurt unskilled labor.[11]

Since the late 1960s, international trade has accounted for an increasing share of the US economy, and beginning in the early 1980s, imports of manufactured goods from developing countries have soared.[12] According to economic theory, the expansion of trade with countries that have a large proportion of relatively unskilled labor will result in downward pressure on the wages of low-skilled Americans because of the lower prices of the goods that those foreign workers produce. Because of the concentration of low-skilled black workers in vulnerable labor-intensive industries (e.g., 40 percent of textile workers are African American, even though blacks make up only about 13 percent of the general population; this overrepresentation is typical in many low-skill industries), developments in international trade are likely to further exacerbate their declining labor market experiences.[13]

Note that the sharp decline in the relative demand for low-skilled labor has had a more adverse effect on blacks than on whites in the United States because a substantially larger proportion of African Americans are unskilled. Indeed, the disproportionate percentage of unskilled African Americans is one of the legacies of historic racial subjugation. Black mobility in the economy was severely impeded by job discrimination, as well as by failing segregated public schools, where per capita expenditures to educate African American children were far below amounts provided for white public schools.[14] While the more educated and highly trained African Americans, like their counterparts among other racial groups, have very likely benefited from the shifts in labor demand, those with lesser skills have suffered. Although the number of skilled blacks (including managers, professionals, and technicians) has increased sharply in the last several years, the proportion of those who are unskilled remains large. This is because the black population, burdened by cumulative experiences of racial restrictions, was overwhelmingly unskilled just several decades ago.[15] As urban economies have transformed from goods production to more of a digitized, information-focused, "virtual" workplace, black central-city residents with little or no education beyond high school see their access to employment increasingly restricted to low-paying jobs in the service sector.

The economic situation for many African Americans has now been further weakened because not only do they tend to reside in communities that have higher jobless rates and lower employment growth—for example, places like Detroit or Philadelphia—but also they lack access to areas of higher employment growth.[16] As the world of corporate employment has relocated to America's suburban communities, over two-thirds of employment growth in metropolitan areas has occurred in the suburbs,[17] many of the residents of our inner-city ghettos have become physically isolated from places of employment and socially isolated from the informal job networks that are often essential for job placement.

The growing suburbanization of jobs means that labor markets today are mainly regional, and long commutes in automobiles are common among blue-collar as well as white-collar workers. For those who cannot afford to own, operate, and insure a private automobile, the commute between inner-city neighborhoods and suburban job locations becomes a Herculean effort.[18] For example, Boston welfare recipients found that only 14 percent of the entry-level jobs in the fast-growth areas of the Boston metropolitan region could be accessed via public transit in less than an hour. And in the Atlanta metropolitan area, fewer than half the entry-level jobs are located within a quarter mile of a public transit system.[19] To make matters worse, many inner-city residents lack information about suburban job opportunities. In the segregated inner-city ghettos, the breakdown of the informal job information network magnifies the problems of *job spatial mismatch*—the notion that work and people are located in two different places.[20]

Although racial discrimination and segregation exacerbate the labor market problems of low-skilled African Americans, many of these problems are currently driven by shifts in the economy.

Between 1947 and the early 1970s, all income groups in America experienced economic advancement. In fact, poor families enjoyed higher growth in annual real income than did other families. In the early 1970s, however, this pattern began to change. American families in higher-income groups, especially those in the top 20 percent, continued to enjoy steady income gains (adjusted for inflation), while those in the lowest 40 percent experienced declining or stagnating incomes. This growing disparity in income, which continued through the mid-1990s, was related to a slowdown in productivity growth and the resulting downward pressure on wages.[21]

Then, beginning in late 1995, productivity began to surge, averaging 2.6 percent annual growth and reaching an astonishing 6.4 percent annual rate in the final quarter of 1999. Given the rate of productivity growth, a rising gross domestic product, and sustained low unemployment rates, the most optimistic scenario at the end of the twentieth century was that this new economy would eventually produce rates of family economic progress similar to those of the 1950s and 1960s.

From 1996 to 2000, *real wage growth*—that is, wages adjusted for inflation—was quite impressive, especially for low-wage workers. The ranks of the *long-term jobless*—defined in the US economy as those in the labor market who have been out of work for more than six months—plummeted from almost 2 million in 1993 to just 637,000 in 2000. The unemployment rate of high school dropouts declined from almost 12 percent in 1992 to less than 7 percent in 2000. The unemployment rate among blacks declined to 7.3 percent, the lowest ever recorded since the Bureau of Labor Statistics began compiling comparable statistics in 1972.

More than any other group, low-skilled workers depend on a strong economy, particularly a sustained tight labor market—that is, one in which there are ample jobs for all applicants. In a slack labor market—a labor market with high unemployment—employers can afford to be more selective in recruiting and granting promotions. With fewer jobs to award, they can inflate job requirements, pursuing workers with college degrees, for example, in jobs that have traditionally been associated with high school–level education. In such an economic climate, discrimination rises and disadvantaged minorities, especially those with low levels of literacy, suffer disproportionately.

Conversely, in a tight labor market, job vacancies are numerous, unemployment is of short duration, and wages are higher. Moreover, in a tight labor market the labor force expands because increased job opportunities not only reduce unemployment but also draw in workers who had previously dropped out of the labor force altogether during a slack labor market period. Thus, in a tight labor market the status of all workers—including disadvantaged minorities—improves.

Just as blacks suffered greatly during the decades of growing separation between haves and have-nots, they benefited considerably from the incredible economic boom that the country enjoyed in the last half of the 1990s.[22] This period saw not only substantially reduced unemployment and concentrated poverty (areas where 40 percent or more of the residents live in poverty) for blacks and other groups, but sharp increases in the earnings of all low-wage workers as well.

Undoubtedly, if the robust economy could have been extended several more years, rather than coming to an abrupt halt in 2001, joblessness and concentrated poverty in inner cities would have declined even more.[23] Nonetheless, many people concerned about poverty and rising inequality have noted that productivity and economic growth are only part of the picture.

Thanks to the Clinton-era economic boom, in the latter 1990s there were signs that the rising economic inequality that had begun in the early 1970s was finally in remission. Nonetheless, worrisome questions were raised by many observers at that time: Would this new economy eventually produce the sort of progress that had prevailed in the two and a half decades prior to 1970—a pattern in which a rising tide had indeed lifted all boats? Or would the government's social and economic policies prevent us from duplicating this prolonged pattern of broadly equal economic gains? In other words, the future of ordinary families, especially poor working families, depends a great deal on how the government decides to react to changes in the economy, and often this reaction has a profound effect on racial outcomes.

In considering the effect of *political* actions that may not be motivated by issues of race, I am reminded of economist James K. Galbraith's observation that what is unique about the 1950s and '60s is that the government's policies—social as well as economic—were integral to the gains experienced by all families. Low-wage workers benefited from a wide range of protections, including steady increases in the minimum wage, and the government made full employment a high priority. Throughout the 1960s these policies were accompanied by federal wage-price guidelines that helped check inflation. In addition, a strong union movement emerged in the 1950s and '60s following the passage of protective legislation in the 1930s and '40s. The activities of unions ensured higher wages and more nonwage benefits for ordinary workers.

In the 1970s and '80s, however, things moved in a different direction for low-wage workers. The union movement began its downward spiral, wage-price guidelines were eventually dropped, and macroeconomic policy was no longer geared toward tight labor markets. Monetary policy came to dominate public policy thinking on the economy, and it was focused on defeating inflation above all else.

The election of Ronald Reagan in 1980 brought to the federal government a new focus on the economy—one in which "supply-side economics" predicted that wealth for the few would eventually "trickle down" as financial well-being for all. As part of the Reagan experiment, the tax structure became more regressive; that is, the proportion of income taxes paid by the wealthy declined while the tax burden was dispersed through a number of other vehicles, including higher Social Security taxes. Furthermore, congressional resistance to raising the minimum wage and to expanding the Earned Income Tax Credit threatened the economic security of disadvantaged families.

During Bill Clinton's eight years in office, redistribution measures were taken to increase the minimum wage. But the George W. Bush administration halted increases in the minimum wage for several years, until the Democrats regained control of Congress in 2006 and voted to again increase the minimum wage in 2007. Thus, many political acts contributed to the decline in real wages experienced by the working poor.[24] Because people of color are disproportionately represented among the working poor, these political acts have reinforced their position in the bottom rungs of the racial stratification ladder. In short, in terms of structural factors that contribute to racial inequality, there are indeed nonracial political forces that must be taken into account.

Understanding the Impact of Cultural Forces

In addition to racial and nonracial structural forces, *cultural* forces may contribute to or reinforce racial inequality. This book examines two types of cultural forces: (1) national views and beliefs on race and (2) cultural traits—shared outlooks, modes of behavior, traditions, belief systems, worldviews, values, skills, preferences, styles of self-presentation, etiquette, and linguistic patterns—that emerge from patterns of intragroup interaction in settings created by discrimination and segregation and that reflect collective experiences within those settings.

I want to avoid limited conceptions of culture defined in the simple and traditional terms of group norms, values, and attitudes toward family and work, and also consider cultural repertoires (habits, styles, and skills) and the micro-level processes of meaning making and decision making—that is, the way individuals in particular groups, communities, or societies develop an understanding of how the world works and make decisions based on that understanding.[25] The processes of meaning making and decision making are reflected in cultural frames (shared group constructions of reality.)

Racism has historically been one of the most prominent American cultural frames and has played a major role in determining how whites perceive and act toward blacks. At its core, racism is an ideology of racial domination with two key features: (1) beliefs that one race is either biologically or culturally inferior to another and (2) the use of such beliefs to rationalize or prescribe the way that the "inferior" race should be treated in this society, as well as to explain its social position as a group and its collective accomplishments. In the United States today, there is no question that the more categorical forms of racist ideology—in particular, those that assert the biogenetic inferiority of blacks—have declined significantly, even though they still may be embedded in institutional norms and practices. For example, school tracking, the practice of grouping students of similar capability for instruction, not only tends to segregate African American students but often results in placing some black students in lower-level classes, even though they have the cultural capital—requisite skills for learning—to compete with students in higher-level classes.[26]

However, there has emerged a form of what Lawrence Bobo and his colleagues refer to as "laissez faire racism," a perception that blacks are responsible for their own economic predicament and therefore undeserving of special government support.[27] The idea that the federal government "has a special obligation to help improve the living standards of blacks" because they "have been discriminated against for so long" was supported by only one in five whites in 2001, and has never exceeded support by more than one in four since 1975. Significantly, the lack of white support for this idea is not related to background factors such as level of education and age.

The vast majority of social scientists agree that, as a national cultural frame, racism in its various forms has had harmful effects on African Americans as a group. Indeed, considerable research has been devoted to the effects of racism in American society. However, there is little research on and far less awareness of the impact of emerging cultural frames in the inner city on the social and economic outcomes of poor blacks. Note that distinct cultural frames in the inner city have not only been shaped by race and poverty, but in turn often shape responses to poverty, including, as we shall soon see, responses that may contribute to the perpetuation of poverty. Moreover, an important research question for social scientists is the following: how much of the framing of racial beliefs at the national level is based on the actual observed cultural traits among the inner-city poor and how much of it is the result of biased media reports and racial stereotypes?

In my own earlier work, I discussed at length how several factors determine the extent to which communities, as areas bounded by place, differ in outlook and behavior.[28] These factors include the degree to which the community is socially isolated from the broader society; the material assets or resources controlled by members of the community; the benefits and privileges the community members derive from these resources; their accumulated cultural experiences from current as well as historical, political, and economic arrangements; and the influence that members of the community wield because of these arrangements.

Culture is closely intertwined with social relations in the sense of providing tools (skills, habits, and styles) and creating constraints (restrictions or limits on behavior or outlooks) in patterns of social interaction.[29] These constraints include cultural frames (shared visions of human behavior) developed over time through the processes of in-group *meaning making* (shared views on how the world works) and *decision making* (choices that reflect shared definitions of how the world works)—for example, in the inner-city ghetto, cultural frames define issues of trust/ street smarts and "acting black" or "acting white"—that lead to observable group characteristics.[30]

One of the effects of living in racially segregated neighborhoods is exposure to group-specific cultural traits (cultural frames, orientations, habits, and worldviews, as well as styles of behavior and particular skills) that emerged from patterns of racial exclusion and that may not be conducive to factors that facilitate social mobility. For example, as revealed in Elijah Anderson's research, some groups in the inner city put a high value on "street smarts," the behaviors and actions that keep them safe in areas of high crime.[31] Street smarts may be an adaptation to living in unsafe neighborhoods. In this environment, it is wise to avoid eye contact with strangers and keep to yourself. This mind-set may also lead someone to approach new situations with a certain level of skepticism or mistrust. Although such an approach is logical and smart in an unsafe neighborhood, the same behavior can be interpreted as antisocial in another setting. Moreover, this street-smart behavior may, in some cases, prevent individuals from performing well on job interviews, creating a perception that they are not desirable job candidates.

Other concrete examples from the writings of both Elijah Anderson and Sudhir Venkatesh on ghetto experiences might prove even more illuminating.[32] Each author reveals the existence of informal rules in the inner-city ghetto that govern interactions and shape how people engage one another and make decisions. This decision making is influenced partly by how people come to view their world over time—what we call "meaning making." It is important to remember that the processes of meaning making and decision making evolve in situations imposed by poverty and racial segregation—situations that place severe constraints on social mobility. Over time, these processes lead to the development of informal codes that regulate behavior.

First of all, Anderson talks about the "code of the street," an informal but explicit set of rules developed to govern interpersonal public behavior and regulate violence in Philadelphia's inner-city ghetto neighborhoods, where crime is high and police protection is low. Anderson argues that the issue of respect is at the root of the code. In a context of limited opportunities for self-actualization and success, some individuals in the community, most notably young black males, devise alternative ways to gain respect that emphasize manly pride, ranging from simply wearing brand-name clothing to have the "right look" and talking the right way, to developing a predatory attitude toward neighbors. Anderson points out, however, that no one residing in these troubled neighborhoods is unaffected by the code of the street—especially young people, who are drawn into this negative culture both on the streets and in the schools as they must frequently adopt "street" behavior as a form of self-defense. As Anderson puts it, "the code of the street is actually a cultural adaptation to a profound lack of faith in the police and the judicial system—and in others who would champion one's personal security."[33]

A related informal but regulated pattern of behavior is described by Sudhir Venkatesh in his study of the underground economy in ghetto neighborhoods. Venkatesh points out that "the underground arena is not simply a place to buy goods and services. It is also a field of social relationships that enable off-the-books trading to occur in an ordered and predictable manner."[34] This trading often results in disagreements or breaches because there are no laws on the books, "but the main point is that in situations ostensibly criminal and often threatening to personal security, there is still a structure in place that shapes how people make decisions and engage one another."[35] In other words, informal rules actually govern what would appear on the surface to be random underground activity. These rules stipulate what is expected of those involved in these informal exchanges and where they should meet. Just as Anderson describes a "code of the street," Venkatesh talks about a "code of shady dealings."

Like Anderson in his effort to explain the emergence of the code of the street, Venkatesh argues that the code of shady dealing is a response to circumstances in inner-city ghetto neighborhoods, where joblessness is high and opportunities for advancement are severely limited. Furthermore, both Anderson and Venkatesh clearly argue that these cultural codes ultimately hinder integration into the broader society and are therefore dysfunctional. In other words, they contribute to the perpetuation of poverty.

Anderson finds that, for some young men, the draw of the street is so powerful that they cannot avail themselves of legitimate employment opportunities when those opportunities become available. Likewise, Venkatesh maintains that adherence to the code of shady dealings impedes social mobility. The "underground economy enables people to survive but can lead to alienation from the wider world," he states.[36] For example, none of the work experience accrued in the informal economy can be listed on résumés for job searches in the formal labor market, and time invested in underground work reduces time devoted to accumulating skills or contacts for legitimate employment.

However, many liberal scholars are reluctant to discuss or research the role that culture plays in the negative outcomes found in the inner city. It is possible that they fear being criticized for reinforcing the popular view that the negative social outcomes—poverty, unemployment, drug addition, crime—of many poor people in the inner city are due to the shortcomings of the people themselves. Indeed, the Harvard University sociologist Orlando Patterson maintains that there is "a deep-seated dogma that has prevailed in social science and policy circles since the mid-1960s: the rejection of any explanation that invokes a group's cultural attributes—its distinctive attitudes, values and tendencies, and the resulting behavior of its members—and the relentless preference for relying on structural factors like low incomes, joblessness, poor schools and bad housing."[37]

Patterson claims that social scientists have shied away from cultural explanations of race and poverty because of the widespread belief that such explanations are tantamount to blaming the victim; that is, they support the conclusion that the poor themselves, and not the social environment, are responsible for their own poverty and negative social outcomes. He colorfully contends that it is "utterly bogus" to argue, as do many academics, that cultural explanations necessarily blame the victim for poor social outcomes. To hold an individual responsible for his behavior is not to rule out any consideration of the environmental factors that may have evoked the questionable behavior to begin with. "Many victims of child abuse end up behaving in self-destructive ways," Patterson states. "To point out the link between their behavior and the destructive acts is in no way to deny the causal role of their earlier victimization and the need to address it."[38] Patterson also contends that a cultural explanation of human behavior not only examines the immediate relationship between attitudes and behavior but also looks at the past to investigate the origins and changing nature of these attitudes.

I agree with Patterson that cultural explanations should be part of any attempt to fully account for such behavior and outcomes. And I think it is equally important to acknowledge that recognizing the important role of cultural influences in creating different racial group outcomes does not require us to ignore or play down the role of structural factors.

The relative importance of cultural or structural explanations in accounting for behaviors and social outcomes is often debatable—though I will argue later that, in terms of major effects on immediate group social outcomes and racial stratification, structure trumps culture. Nevertheless, I firmly believe that to apply these explanations totally separately, without any attempt to show how they interact, is indeed a mistake. Moreover, if we are going to examine social and economic factors that, over time, contributed to the development of certain cultural traits and related behavior, we must also pay serious attention to the immediate impact of structural conditions.

I also strongly agree with Orlando Patterson that an adequate explanation of cultural attributes in the black community must explore the origins and changing nature of attitudes and practices going back decades, even centuries. Unfortunately, such analyses are complex and difficult.[39] It took years of research by Kathryn Neckerman to provide the historical evidence to explain why so many black youngsters and their parents lose faith in public schools. Neckerman shows in her book *Schools Betrayed* that a century ago, when African American children in most northern cities attended schools alongside white children, the problems commonly associated with inner-city schools—low achievement and high dropout rates—were not nearly as pervasive as they are today.[40]

Neckerman carefully documents how city officials responded to increases in the African American student population: by introducing and enforcing segregation between black and white children in the city schools. And she discusses at length how poor, white immigrant children—whose family circumstances were at least as impoverished as their black counterparts—received more and better resources for their education. Over the course of sixty years, then, generations of children of black Chicagoans were denied the opportunities that their white counterparts were able to expect from the public school system.

Although most people today understand the suppression of black aspiration that occurred in the Jim Crow South, few realize that this tradition of school segregation persisted in northern cities, as Neckerman's book so aptly documents. "The roots of classroom alienation, antagonism, and disorder can be found in school policy decisions made long before the problems of inner-city schools attracted public attention," states Neckerman. "These policies struck at the foundations of authority and engagement, making it much more difficult for inner-city teachers to gain student cooperation in learning. The district's history of segregation and inequality undermined the schools' legitimacy in the eyes of its black students; as a result, inner-city teachers struggled to gain cooperation from children and parents, who had little reason to trust the school."[41] Clearly, we can more fully understand the frustration and current cultural dynamics in inner-city neighborhoods, in this case with reference to public schools, if we understand the history that work like Neckerman's uncovers.

Finally, although culture "partly determines behavior, it also enables people to change behavior."[42] Culture provides a frame for individuals to understand their world. And I agree that, by ignoring or investigating culture at only a superficial level, social scientists miss an opportunity to help people understand and then reframe attitudes in a way that promotes desirable behavior and outcomes.[43]

However, attitudes must be reframed in conjunction with programs that address structural inequities. For example, take the problem of black male fatherhood that we will explore in greater detail in Chapter 3. I would argue that programs focusing on the cultural problems pertaining to fatherhood, including attitudes concerning paternity, without confronting the broader and more fundamental issues of restricted economic opportunities, have limited chances to succeed. In my view, the most effective fatherhood programs in the inner city will be those that address the framing of attitudes, norms, and behaviors in combination with local and national attempts to improve job prospects. Only when black fathers have a realistic opportunity to adequately care for their children financially will they be able to envision a more family-centered life for themselves and their children.

Conclusion

For many years, social scientists and other observers and analysts have debated the role of social structure versus culture in explaining the social and economic outcomes of African Americans, including their educational attainment and success in the labor market. The position taken often reflects ideological bias. Conservatives tend to emphasize cultural factors, while liberals pay more attention to structural conditions, with most of the attention devoted to racialist structural factors such as discrimination and segregation. I hope in this discussion, however, to encourage the development of a framework for understanding the formation and maintenance of racial inequality and racial group outcomes that integrates cultural factors with two types of structural forces: those that directly reflect explicit racial bias and those that do not.

In the ensuing chapters I apply this framework to three topics pertaining to the inner-city African American experience that have generated the most intense debates: the formation and persistence of the inner-city ghetto, the plight of black males, and the breakdown of the black family. Naturally, in this process I raise some warning flags about incorporating cultural arguments into our analysis of race and poverty that we should not ignore. Nevertheless, the long-standing problem of race in the United States calls for a bold, new perspective. I hope to pursue such a perspective in the chapters that follow.

CHAPTER 2

THE FORCES SHAPING CONCENTRATED POVERTY

T hrough the second half of the 1990s and into the early years of the twenty-first century, public attention to the plight of poor black Americans seemed to wane. There was scant media attention to the problem of concentrated urban poverty (neighborhoods in which a high percentage of the residents fall beneath the federally designated poverty line), little or no discussion of inner-city challenges by mainstream political leaders, and even an apparent quiescence on the part of ghetto residents themselves. This situation was dramatically different from the 1960s, when the transition from legal segregation to a more racially open society had been punctuated by social unrest that sometimes expressed itself in violent terms, as seen in the riots that followed the assassination of Dr. Martin Luther King Jr.

In 2005, however, Hurricane Katrina exposed concentrated

poverty in New Orleans. When television cameras focused on the flooding, the people trapped in houses and apartments, and the vast devastation, many Americans were shocked to see the squalid living conditions of the poor. Of course, the devastation of Katrina was broadly visited upon the residents of New Orleans—black and white, rich and poor, property owner and public housing tenant alike. But although many residents were able to flee, the very poor, lacking automobiles or money for transportation and lodging, stayed to wait out the storm, with tragic results. And through Katrina, the nation's attention became riveted to these poor urban neighborhoods.

Some people argued that Katrina demonstrated how foolhardy it is to rely on the government for protection rather than on oneself and control of one's own fate. However, it is unfair and indeed unwarranted to blame people with limited resources for being trapped in their neighborhoods and vulnerable to natural disasters. People who reside in these poor, ghetto neighborhoods include not only those on public assistance, but also the working poor, many of whom have never been on welfare.

The fact that many families in the inner city of New Orleans were trapped there during Katrina because they did not have access to automobiles and other means of transportation is a problem that is not unique to New Orleans. For example, research conducted in the Chicago inner-city ghetto areas revealed that only 19 percent of the residents have access to an automobile.[1] A person in these segregated and highly concentrated poverty areas could be very disciplined and responsible, working every day for minimum wages and barely making ends meet, in no position to buy and maintain an automobile; and by virtue of his or her low income, that person would be completely dependent on public transportation. No one in such a situation could quickly relocate his or her family to other areas.

If television cameras had focused on the urban poor in New Orleans, or on any inner-city ghetto, before Katrina, I believe that the initial reaction to descriptions of poverty and poverty concentration would have been unsympathetic. Public opinion polls in the United States, as we shall soon see, routinely reflect the notion that people are poor and jobless because of their own shortcomings or inadequacies. In other words, few people would have reflected on how the larger forces in society—segregation, discrimination, a lack of economic opportunity, failing public schools—adversely affect the inner-city poor. However, because Katrina was clearly a natural disaster beyond the control of the inner-city poor, Americans were much more sympathetic. In a sense, Katrina turned out to be something of a cruel natural experiment, wherein better-off Americans could readily see the effects of racial isolation and chronic economic subordination.

Despite the lack of national public awareness of the problems of the urban poor prior to Katrina, social scientists have rightly devoted considerable attention to concentrated poverty because it magnifies the problems associated with poverty in general: joblessness, crime, delinquency, drug trafficking, broken families, and dysfunctional schools. Neighborhoods of highly concentrated poverty are seen as dangerous, and therefore they become isolated, socially and economically, as people go out of their way to avoid them.[2]

If social scientists are to effectively and comprehensively explain the experiences and social outcomes of inner-city residents to the larger public, they must consider not only how explicit racial structural forces directly contribute to inequality and concentrated poverty, but also how *political actions* and impersonal *economic forces* indirectly affect life in the inner city. Also important are the effects of national racial beliefs and cultural constraints that have emerged from years of racial isolation and chronic economic subordination.

The Role of Political Actions

Ever since 1934, with the establishment of the Federal Housing Administration (FHA), a program necessitated by the massive mortgage foreclosures during the Great Depression, the US government has sought to enable citizens to become home owners by underwriting mortgages. In the years following World War II, however, the federal government contributed to the early decay of inner-city neighborhoods by withholding mortgage capital and making it difficult for these areas to retain or attract families who were able to purchase their own homes. Spurred on by the massive foreclosures during the Great Depression, the federal government began underwriting mortgages in an effort to enable citizens to become home owners. But the FHA selectively administered the mortgage program by formalizing a process that excluded certain urban neighborhoods by using empirical data that suggested a likely loss of investment in these areas.

Redlining, as this practice came to be known, was assessed largely on racial composition. Although many neighborhoods with a considerable number of European immigrants were redlined, virtually all black neighborhoods were excluded. Home buyers hoping to purchase a home in a redlined neighborhood were universally denied mortgages, regardless of their financial qualifications. This practice severely restricted opportunities for building or even maintaining quality housing in the inner city, which in many ways set the stage for the urban blight that many Americans associate with black neighborhoods. This action was clearly motivated by racial bias, and it was not until the 1960s that the FHA discontinued mortgage restrictions based on the racial composition of the neighborhood.[3]

Subsequent policy decisions worked to trap blacks in these

increasingly unattractive inner cities. Beginning in the 1950s, the suburbanization of the middle class, already under way with government-subsidized loans to veterans, was aided further by federal transportation and highway policies, which included the building of freeway networks through the hearts of many cities. Although these policies were seemingly nonracial, the line here between ostensibly nonracial and explicitly racial is gray. For example, we might ask whether such freeways would have also been constructed though wealthier white neighborhoods.

In any case, the freeways had a devastating impact on the neighborhoods of black Americans. These developments not only spurred relocation from the cities to the suburbs among better-off residents, but the freeways themselves "created barriers between the sections of the cities, walling off poor and minority neighborhoods from central business districts."[4] For instance, a number of studies revealed how Richard J. Daley, the former mayor of Chicago, used the Federal-Aid Highway Act of 1956 to route expressways through impoverished African American neighborhoods, resulting in even greater segregation and isolation.[5] A lasting legacy of that policy is the fourteen-lane Dan Ryan Expressway, which created a barrier between black and white neighborhoods.[6]

Another particularly egregious example of the deleterious effects of highway construction is Birmingham, Alabama's, interstate highway system, which curved and twisted to bisect several black neighborhoods rather than taking a more direct route through some predominantly white neighborhoods. The highway system essentially followed the boundaries that had been established in 1926 as part of the city's racial zoning law, although these boundaries technically had been removed a few years before the highway construction began in 1956.[7] Other examples include the federal and state highway system in Atlanta, Georgia, which also separated white and black neighborhoods; and the construction of

I-95 in Florida, which displaced many black residents in Miami's historically black Overtown neighborhood.[8]

Moreover, through its housing-market incentives, the federal government drew middle-class whites away from cities and into the suburbs.[9] Government policies such as mortgages for veterans and mortgage-interest tax exemptions for developers enabled the quick, cheap production of massive amounts of tract housing.[10] Although these policies appeared to be nonracial, they facilitated the exodus of white working and middle-class families from urban neighborhoods and thereby indirectly contributed to the growth of segregated neighborhoods with high concentrations of poverty.

A classic example of this effect of housing-market incentives is the mass-produced suburban Levittown neighborhoods that were first erected in New York, and later in Pennsylvania, New Jersey, and Puerto Rico, by Levitt & Sons. The homes in these neighborhoods were manufactured on a large scale, with an assembly-line model of production, and they were arranged in carefully engineered suburban neighborhoods that included many public amenities, such as shopping centers and space for public schools. These neighborhoods represented an ideal alternative for people seeking to escape cramped city apartments, and they were often touted as "utopian communities" that enabled people to live out the "suburban dream." Veterans were able to purchase a Levittown home for a few thousand dollars with no money down, financed with low-interest mortgages guaranteed by the Veterans Administration. However, initially the Levitts would not sell to African Americans. The first black family moved into the New York Levittown neighborhood in 1957, having purchased a home from a white family,[11] and they endured harassment, hate mail, and threats for several months after moving in. Levittown, New York, remains a predominantly white community today. Here, once again, we see a practice that denied African Americans the opportunity to move from segregated inner-city neighborhoods.

Explicit racial policies in the suburbs reinforced this segregation by allowing suburbs to separate their financial resources and municipal budgets from cities. To be more specific, in the nineteenth and early twentieth centuries, strong municipal services in cities were very attractive to residents of small towns and suburbs; as a result, cities tended to annex suburbs and surrounding areas. But the relations between cities and suburbs in the United States began to change following the Great Depression; the century-long influx of poor migrants who required expensive services and paid relatively little in taxes could no longer be profitably absorbed by the city economy. Annexation largely ended in the mid-twentieth century as suburbs began to successfully resist incorporation. Suburban communities also drew tighter boundaries by implementing zoning laws, discriminatory land use controls, and site selection practices, which made it difficult for inner-city racial minorities to access these areas because they were effectively used to screen out residents on the basis of race.

As separate political jurisdictions, suburbs also exercised a great deal of autonomy through covenants and deed restrictions. In the face of mounting pressure for integration in the 1960s, "suburbs chose to diversify by race rather than class. They retained zoning and other restrictions that allowed only affluent blacks (and in some instances Jews) to enter, thereby intensifying the concentration and isolation of the urban poor."[12] Although these policies clearly had racial connotations, they also reflected class bias and helped reinforce a process already amply supported by federal government policies—namely, the exodus of white working- and middle-class families from urban neighborhoods and the growing segregation of low-income blacks in inner-city neighborhoods.

Federal public housing policy contributed to the gradual growth of segregated black ghettos as well. The federal public housing program's policies evolved in two stages that represented two distinct styles. The Wagner-Steagall Housing Act of 1937 initiated the first stage. Concerned that the construction of public housing might depress private rent levels, groups such as the US Building and Loan League and the National Association of Real Estate Boards successfully lobbied Congress to require, by law, that for each new unit of public housing, one "unsafe or unsanitary" unit of public housing be destroyed. As Mark Condon points out, "this policy increased employment in the urban construction market while insulating private rent levels by barring the expansion of the housing stock available to low-income families."[13]

The early years of the public housing program produced positive results. Initially, the program served mainly intact families temporarily displaced by the Depression or in need of housing after the end of World War II. For many of these families, public housing was the first step on the road toward economic recovery. Their stays in the projects were relatively brief because they were able to accumulate sufficient economic resources to move on to private housing. The economic mobility of these families "contributed to the sociological stability of the first public housing communities, and explains the program's initial success."[14]

Passage of the Housing Act of 1949 marked the beginning of the second policy stage. It instituted and funded the urban renewal program designed to eradicate urban slums and therefore was seemingly nonracial. However, the public housing that it created "was now meant to collect the ghetto residents left homeless by the urban renewal bulldozers."[15] A new (lower) income ceiling for public housing residency was established by the federal public housing authority, and families with incomes above that ceiling were evicted. Thus, access to public housing was restricted to only the most economically disadvantaged segments of the population.

This change in federal housing policy coincided with the Second Great Migration of African Americans from the rural South to the cities of the Northeast and Midwest, which lasted thirty years—from 1940 to 1970. This mass movement of African Americans was even larger and more sustained than the first Great Migration, which began at the turn of the twentieth century and ended during the Great Depression, and it had a more profound impact on the transformation of the inner city.

As the black urban population in the North grew and precipitated greater demands for housing, pressure mounted in white communities to keep blacks out. Suburban communities, with their restrictive covenants and special zoning laws, refused to permit the construction of public housing. And the federal government acquiesced to organized white inner-city groups that opposed the construction of public housing in their neighborhoods. Thus, public housing units were overwhelmingly concentrated in the overcrowded and deteriorating inner-city ghettos—the poorest and least powerful sections of the city and the metropolitan area. "This growing population of politically weak urban poor was unable to counteract the desires of vocal middle- and working-class whites for segregated housing,"[16] housing that would keep blacks out of white neighborhoods. In short, public housing became a federally funded institution that isolated families by race and class, resulting in high concentrations of poor black families in inner-city ghettos.[17]

In the last quarter of the twentieth century, new developments led to further changes in these neighborhoods. One of the most significant was the out-migration of middle-income blacks. Before the 1970s, African American families had faced extremely strong barriers when they considered moving into white neighborhoods. Not only did many experience overt discrimination in the housing market, but some were victims of violent attacks. Although fair-housing audits continue to reveal the existence of discrimination in the housing market, the fair-housing legislation, including the Fair Housing Amendments Act of 1988, reduced the strengths of these barriers. And middle-income African Americans increased their efforts to move from concentrated black poverty areas to more desirable neighborhoods in the metropolitan area, including white neighborhoods.[18]

This pattern represents an important change in the formation of neighborhoods. In earlier years, communities undergoing racial change from white to black had tended to experience an increase in population density, as a result of the black migration from the South. Because of the housing demand, particularly in the late stages of the succession from white to black, homes and apartments in these neighborhoods were often subdivided into smaller units.[19]

However, 1970 marked the end of the great migration wave of blacks from the South to northern urban areas, and two developments affected the course of population movement to the inner cities after that. Improvements in transportation made it easier for workers to live outside the central city, and industries gradually shifted to the suburbs because of the increased residential suburbanization of the labor force and the lower cost of production. Because of the suburbanization of employment and improvements in transportation, inner-city manufacturing jobs were no longer a strong factor pulling migrants to central cities.[20]

With the decline of industrial employment in the inner city, the influx of southern blacks to northern cities ceased and many poor black neighborhoods, especially those in the Midwest and Northeast, changed from densely packed areas of recently arrived migrants to communities gradually abandoned by the working and middle classes.[21]

In addition, and more recently, a fundamental shift in the federal government's support for basic urban programs profoundly aggravated the problems of inner-city neighborhoods. Beginning in 1980, when Ronald Reagan became president, sharp spending cuts on direct aid to cities dramatically reduced budgets for general revenue sharing—unrestricted funds (money that can be used for any purpose)—urban mass transit, economic development assistance, urban development action grants, social service block grants, local public works, compensatory education, public service jobs, and job training. Many of these programs are designed to help disadvantaged individuals gain some traction in attaining financial security.[22] It is telling that the federal contribution was 17.5 percent of the total city budgets in 1977, but only 5.4 percent by 2000.[23]

These cuts were particularly acute for older cities in the East and Midwest that depended largely on federal and state aid to fund social services for their poor populations and to maintain aging infrastructure. In 1980, for example, federal and state aid funded 50 to 69 percent of the budgets in six of these cities, and 40 to 50 percent of budgets in eleven other cities. By 1989, only three cities—Buffalo, Baltimore, and Newark—continued to receive over 50 percent of their budgets in state aid; and only two cities—Milwaukee and Boston—received between 40 and 50 percent of their budgets in state aid. To illustrate further, New York City's state aid dropped from 52 percent of its budget in 1980 to 32 percent in 1989, resulting in a loss of $4 billion.[24] Here, once again, is a policy that is nonracial on the surface—although it coincided with changes in the proportion of white and nonwhite urban residents—but nonetheless has indirectly contributed to crystallization of the inner-city ghetto.

The decline in federal support for cities since 1980 coincided with an increase in the immigration of people from poorer countries—mainly low-skilled workers from Mexico—and the steady migration of whites to the suburbs. With minorities displacing whites as a growing share of the central-city population, the implications for the urban tax base were profound, especially in America's cities. According to the US Census Bureau, in 2000 the median annual household income for Latinos was about $14,000 less than that of white households. With a declining tax base and the simultaneous loss of federal funds that heralded the introduction of the New Federalist policies of the Reagan administration, municipalities had trouble raising enough revenue to cover basic services such as garbage collection, street cleaning, and police protection. Some even cut such services in order to avoid bankruptcy.[25]

This financial crisis left many cities ill equipped to handle three devastating public health problems that had emerged in the 1980s and had disproportionately affected areas of concentrated poverty: (1) the prevalence of drug trafficking and associated violent crimes; (2) the AIDS epidemic and its escalating public health costs; and (3) the rise in the homeless population not only of individuals, but of whole families as well.[26] Although drug addiction, drug-related violence, AIDS, and homelessness are found in many American communities, their impact on the black ghetto is profound. A number of cities, especially fiscally strapped cities, have watched helplessly as these problems—aggravated by the reduction of citywide social services, as well as high levels of neighborhood joblessness—have reinforced the perception that cities are dangerous and threatening places to live. Accordingly, between the 1980s and 2000, many working- and middle-class urban residents continued to relocate to the suburbs. Thus, while poverty and joblessness, and the social problems they generate, remain prominent in ghetto neighborhoods, many cities have fewer and fewer resources to combat them.

Although fiscal conditions in many cities improved significantly in the latter half of the 1990s, this brief period of economic progress was ended by the recession of 2001, followed by a jobless recovery (i.e., a recovery that failed to improve the employment rate). The decline of federal and state support for central cities, the largest urban areas in metropolitan regions, has caused a number of severe fiscal and service crises, particularly in the older cities of the East and Midwest, such as Detroit, Cleveland, Baltimore, and Philadelphia.

Moreover, the George W. Bush administration's substantial reductions in federal aid to the states exacerbated the problems in cities reliant on state funds.[27] Because of these combined economic and political changes, many central cities and inner suburbs lack the fiscal means to address the concentrated problems of joblessness, family breakups, and failing public schools.[28] Given the current budget deficit—which continues to grow in the face of the Bush administration's simultaneous surrender of revenue in the form of large tax cuts for wealthy citizens and its spending of billions of federal dollars to pay for the wars in Iraq and Afghanistan, the war against terror, and the rebuilding of Iraq's infrastructure—support for programs to revitalize cities in general and inner-city neighborhoods in particular will very likely garner even less support from policy makers in the future.[29]

Finally, policy makers indirectly contributed to concentrated poverty in inner-city neighborhoods with decisions that decreased the attractiveness of low-paying jobs and accelerated the relative decline in low-income workers' wages. In particular, in the absence of an effective labor market policy, policy makers tolerated industry practices that undermine worker security—including the erosion of benefits and the rise of involuntary part-time employment—and they allowed the purchasing power of the federal minimum wage to erode to one of its lowest levels in decades. After adjusting for inflation, the current federal minimum wage of $6.55 is 24 percent lower than the average level of the minimum wage in the 1960s, 23 percent lower than in the 1970s, 6 percent lower than in the 1980s, and only 1 percent higher than in the 1990s.[30] Clearly, the recent action by a Democratic Congress to increase the federally mandated minimum wage was long overdue.

In sum, federal government policies, even those that are not explicitly racial, have had a profound impact on inner-city neighborhoods. Some of these policies are clearly motivated by racial bias, such as the FHA's redlining of black neighborhoods in the 1940s and 1950s, as well as the federal government's decision to confine construction of public housing projects mainly to inner-city, poor, black neighborhoods. In other cases it seems that racial bias or concerns about race influenced but were not the sole inspiration for political decisions, such as the fiscal policies of the New Federalism, which resulted in drastic cuts in federal aid to cities whose populations had become more brown and black.

The point of conservative fiscal policy—no matter whose administration promulgated it (Reagan, George H. W. Bush, or George W. Bush)—was ostensibly to subject government to financial discipline. Nevertheless, the enactment of such policies creates financial constraints that make it difficult to generate the political support to effectively combat problems such as joblessness, drug trafficking, AIDS, family stress, and failing schools.

Furthermore, as we have seen already, other policies that range from those that clearly lack a racial agenda to those where the line between racial and nonracial is somewhat gray have had a profound impact on inner cities and their poor black residents: Federal transportation and highway policy created an infrastructure for jobs in the suburbs. Mortgage-interest tax exemptions and mortgages for veterans jointly facilitated the exodus of working-

and middle-class white families from inner-city neighborhoods. Urban renewal and the building of freeway and highway networks through the hearts of many cities led to the destruction of many viable low-income black neighborhoods. And there were no effective labor market policies to safeguard the real value of the minimum wage, thereby making it more difficult for the inner-city working poor to support their families.

These developments have occurred in many cities across the country, but they perhaps have been felt more in the older central cities of the Midwest and Northeast—the traditional Rust Belt— where depopulated poverty areas have experienced even greater problems.

The Impact of Economic Forces

Older urban areas were once the hubs of economic growth and activity and therefore major destinations for people in search of economic opportunity. However, the economies of many of these cities have since been eroded by complex economic transformations and shifting patterns in metropolitan development. These economic forces are typically considered nonracial—in the sense that their origins are not the direct result of actions, processes, or ideologies that explicitly reflect racial bias. But nevertheless they have accelerated neighborhood decline in the inner city and widened gaps in race and income between cities and suburbs.[31]

As I mentioned in Chapter 1, since the mid-twentieth century the mode of production in the United States has shifted dramatically from manufacturing to one increasingly fueled by finance, services, and technology. This shift has accompanied the technological revolution, which has transformed traditional industries and brought about changes ranging from streamlined information technology to biomedical engineering.[32]

In other words, the relationship between technology and international competition has eroded the basic institutions of the mass production system. In the last several decades almost all improvements in productivity have been associated with technology and human capital, thereby drastically reducing the importance of physical capital.[33] With the increased globalization of economic activity, firms have spread their operations around the world, often relocating their production facilities to developing nations that have dramatically lower labor costs.[34]

These global economic transformations have adversely affected the competitive position of many US Rust Belt cities. For example, Cleveland, Detroit, Philadelphia, Baltimore, and Pittsburgh perform poorly on employment growth, an important traditional measure of economic performance. Nationally, employment increased by 25 percent between 1991 and 2001, yet job growth in these older central cities either declined or did not exceed 3 percent.[35]

With the decline in manufacturing employment in many of the nation's central cities, most of the jobs for lower-skilled workers are now in retail and service industries (e.g., store cashiers, customer service representatives, fast-food servers, custodial workers). Whereas jobs in manufacturing industries were unionized, were relatively stable, and carried higher wages, those for workers with low to modest levels of education in the retail and service industries provided lower wages, tended to be unstable, and lacked the benefits and worker protections—such as workers' health insurance, medical leave, retirement benefits, and paid vacations—typically offered through unionization. Thus, workers relegated to low-wage service and retail firms are more likely to experience hardships as they struggle to make ends meet. In addition, the local economy suffers when residents have fewer dollars to spend in their neighborhoods.[36]

Beginning in the mid-1970s, the employment balance between central cities and suburbs shifted markedly to the suburbs. Since 1980, over two-thirds of employment growth has occurred outside the central city: manufacturing is now over 70 percent suburban, and wholesale and retail trade is just under 70 percent suburban.[37] The suburbs of many central cities, developed originally as bedroom localities for commuters to the central business and manufacturing districts, have become employment centers in themselves. In Detroit, Philadelphia, and Baltimore, for example, less than 20 percent of the jobs are now located within three miles of the city center.[38]

Accompanying the rise of suburban and exurban economies has been a change in commuting patterns. Increasingly, workers completely bypass the central city by commuting from one suburb to another. "In the Cleveland region, for example, less than one-third of workers commute to a job in the central city and over half (55 percent) begin and end in the suburbs."[39]

Sprawl and economic stagnation reduce inner-city residents' access to meaningful economic opportunities and thereby fuel the economic decline of their neighborhoods. *Spatial mismatch* is a term that social scientists use to capture the relationship between inner-city residents and suburban jobs: the opportunities for employment are geographically disconnected from the people who need the jobs. In Cleveland, for example, although entry-level workers are concentrated in inner-city neighborhoods, 80 percent of the entry-level jobs are located in the suburbs.[40] The lack of feasible transportation options exacerbates this mismatch. In addition to the challenges in learning about and reaching jobs, there is persistent racial discrimination in hiring practices, especially for younger and less experienced minority workers.[41]

With the departure of higher-income families, the least upwardly mobile individuals in society—mainly low-income people of color—are left behind in neighborhoods with high concentrations of poverty and deteriorating physical conditions. These neighborhoods offer few jobs and typically lack basic services and amenities, such as banks, grocery stores and other retail establishments, parks, and quality transit.[42] Typically, these communities also suffer from substandard schools, many with run-down physical plants.

Two of the most visible indicators of neighborhood decline are abandoned buildings and vacant lots. According to one recent report, there are 60,000 abandoned and vacant properties in Philadelphia, 40,000 in Detroit, and 26,000 in Baltimore.[43] These inner-city properties have lost residents in the wake of the out-migration of more economically mobile families, and the relocation of many manufacturing industries.[44]

The Role of Cultural Factors

Even though these structural changes have adversely affected inner-city neighborhoods, there is a widespread notion in America that the problems plaguing people in the inner city have little to do with racial discrimination or the effects of living in segregated poverty. For many Americans, the individual and the family bear the main responsibility for their low social and economic achievement in society. If unchallenged, this view may suggest that cultural traits are at the root of problems experienced by the ghetto poor.

As I pointed out in Chapter 1, culture provides tools (habits, skills, and styles) and creates constraints (restrictions or limits on outlooks and behavior) in patterns of social interaction. These constraints include cultural frames (shared group constructions of reality) that influence or direct social action, and, as I shall demonstrate more specifically in Chapters 3 and 4, that action may reinforce racial inequality. It is important to remember that one of the effects of living in a racially segregated, poor neighborhood is the exposure to cultural framing, habits, styles of behavior, and particular skills that emerged from patterns of racial exclusion; these attributes and practices may not be conducive to facilitating social mobility. For example, as we shall discuss in Chapter 3, some social scientists have discussed the negative effects of a "cool-pose culture" that has emerged among young black men in the inner city, which includes making sexual conquests, hanging out on the street after school, taking party drugs, and listening to hip-hop music. These patterns of behavior are seen as a hindrance to social mobility in the larger society.[45]

The use of a cultural argument, however, is not without peril. Anyone who wishes to understand American society must be aware that explanations focusing on the cultural traits of inner-city residents are likely to draw far more attention from policy makers and the general public than structural explanations will. It is an unavoidable fact that Americans tend to deemphasize the structural origins and social significance of poverty and welfare. In other words, the popular view is that people are poor or on welfare because of their own personal shortcomings. Perhaps this tendency is rooted in our tradition of "rugged individualism." If, in America, you can grow up to be anything you want to be, then any destiny—even poverty—can be rightly viewed through the lens of personal achievement or failure. Certainly it's true that most Americans have little direct knowledge or understanding of the complex nature of race and poverty in the inner city, and therefore broadly based cultural explanations that focus on personal character are more likely to gain acceptance.

We can easily see that explanations focusing on the character and capabilities of the individual dominate American thinking. Consider studies of national public opinion. After analyzing national survey data collected in 1969 and 1980, James R. Kluegel and Eliot R. Smith concluded that "most Americans believe that opportunity for economic advancement is widely available, that economic outcomes are determined by individuals' efforts and talents (or their lack) and that in general economic inequality is fair."[46] Indeed, responses to questions in these two national American surveys revealed that individualistic explanations for poverty (e.g., lack of effort or ability, poor moral character, slack work skills) were overwhelmingly favored over structural explanations (e.g., lack of adequate schooling, low wages, lack of jobs). The most frequently selected items in the surveys were "lack of thrift or proper money management skills," "lack of effort," "lack of ability or talent" (attitudes from one's family background that impede social mobility); "failure of society to provide good schools"; and "loose morals and drunkenness." Except for "failure of society to provide good schools," all of these phrases point to shortcomings on the part of individuals as the causes of poverty. The Americans who answered the survey considered structural factors, such as "low wages," "failure of industry to provide jobs," and "racial discrimination" least important of all. The rankings of these factors remained virtually unchanged between 1969 and 1980.

A 1990 survey using these same questions, reported by Lawrence Bobo and Ryan A. Smith, revealed a slight increase among those who associate poverty with institutional and structural causes, especially the "failure of industry to provide enough jobs."[47] Nonetheless, Americans remained strongly disposed to the idea that individuals are largely responsible for their economic situations. In the three times the survey was administered—1969, 1980, and 1990—the most often selected explanation was "lack of effort by the poor themselves." In fact, across all three surveys, more than nine out of ten American adults felt that lack of effort was either very or somewhat important in terms of causing poverty. Fewer than 10 percent felt it was not important.

The weight Americans give to individualistic factors persists today. A 2007 survey by the Pew Research Center revealed that "fully two-thirds of all Americans believe personal factors, rather than racial discrimination, explain why many African Americans have difficulty getting ahead in life; just 19% blame discrimination."[48] Nearly three-fourths of US whites (71 percent), a majority of Hispanics (59 percent), and even a slight majority of blacks (53 percent) "believe that blacks who have not gotten ahead in life are mainly responsible for their own situation."[49]

These findings on the importance of individualistic causes of poverty contrast sharply with those in a survey conducted in twelve European countries (England, Ireland, France, Belgium, Holland, Switzerland, Germany, Norway, Sweden, Luxembourg, Austria, and Italy) in 1990.[50] A substantial majority of the citizens in each of these countries favored structural over individual explanations for the causes of poverty and joblessness in their own nations. Given the rising ethnic and racial tensions between host populations and migrants of color from Asia, Africa, and the Middle East, we might have expected these attitudes to shift closer to those held by Americans. However, a 2007 survey of twenty-seven European Union member states revealed that only one in five European Union citizens supported the idea that people live in poverty because of "laziness and lack of will power." Thirty-seven percent viewed "injustice in society as the cause of poverty," 20 percent attributed the cause to "bad luck," and 13 percent found poverty "an inevitable part of progress."[51] The attitudes of ordinary European citizens and public rhetoric in the European Union focus much more on structural and social inequities at large, not on individual behavior, to explain the causes of poverty and joblessness. Obviously, citizens in other Western democracies do not share the American emphasis on individualistic explanations for the problems of poverty.

The strength of American cultural sentiment that individuals are primarily responsible for poverty presents a dilemma for anyone who seeks the most comprehensive explanation of outcomes for poor black Americans. Why? Simply because cultural arguments that focus on individual traits and behavior invariably draw more attention than do structural explanations in the United States. Accordingly, I feel that a social scientist has an obligation to try to make sure that the explanatory power of his or her structural argument is not lost to the reader and to provide a context for understanding cultural responses to chronic economic and racial subordination.

Let me pursue this idea by first considering the neighborhood-effects research that focuses on concentrated poverty. Hundreds of studies have been published on the effects of concentrated poverty in neighborhood environments since the late 1980s. The research suggests that concentrated poverty increases the likelihood of social isolation (from mainstream institutions), joblessness, dropping out of school, lower educational achievement, involvement in crime, unsuccessful behavioral development and delinquency among adolescents, nonmarital childbirth, and unsuccessful family management.[52] In general, the research reveals that concentrated poverty adversely affects one's chances in life, beginning in early childhood and adolescence.

Some scholars, however, have been concerned that these studies reached conclusions about neighborhood effects on the basis of data that do not address the problem of *self-selection bias*, a term used in research to describe the effect of people grouping themselves together according to common characteristics. Proponents of self-selection bias argue that the effects we attribute to poor neighborhoods may instead be caused by the characteristics of families and individuals who end up living there. In other words, they believe that disadvantaged neighborhoods might not be the cause of poor outcomes, but rather that families with the weakest job-related skills, with the lowest awareness of and concern for the effects of the local environment on their children's social development, with attitudes that hinder social mobility, and with the most burdensome personal problems are simply more likely to live in these types of neighborhoods.

For example, as John Quigley and Steven Raphael point out, "in interpreting cross-sectional data on the isolation of low-income workers from job concentrations, it is likely that those with weaker attachments to the labor force will have chosen to locate in places where employment access is low [e.g., inner-city ghetto neighborhoods]. This is simply because monthly rents are lower in these places."[53]

Indeed, some scholars maintain that neighborhood effects disappear when researchers use appropriate statistical techniques to account for self-selection bias.[54] Because the appropriateness of measures capturing neighborhood effects is not discussed as a major problem in such studies, a point that I will soon discuss, many readers will conclude that structural explanations of concentrated poverty and related problems like discrimination, segregation, and joblessness are less persuasive than those that focus on personal attributes. But, as I shall attempt to show, there is little basis for ignoring or downplaying neighborhood effects in favor of emphasizing personal attributes. Indeed, living in a ghetto neighborhood has both structural and cultural effects that compromise life chances above and beyond personal attributes.

Arguments about self-selection bias were not seen as seriously challenging conclusions about neighborhood effects until publication of the research on the Moving to Opportunity (MTO) experiment, a housing pilot program undertaken by the US Department of Housing and Urban Development (HUD) between 1994 and 1998. The MTO program was inspired by the Gautreaux program, an earlier effort to assist minorities who wished to leave the inner city. The Gautreaux program was created under a 1976 court order resulting from a judicial finding that the Chicago Housing Authority had deliberately segregated black families through its site selection and tenant selection policies and the US Department of Housing and Urban Development (HUD) had knowingly funded such violations of civil rights. Named for Dorothy Gautreaux, who initiated the original lawsuit, the program sought to remedy previous segregation by offering black public housing residents a chance to obtain subsidized housing throughout the greater Chicago area. By the time the Gautreaux program ended in 1998, it had placed 7,100 families, with over half relocating to white suburbs.

As the program unfolded, it allowed researchers to systematically compare the education and employment experiences of families who had been assigned to private subsidized housing in the suburbs with those of a comparison group with similar characteristics and history who had been assigned to private apartments in the city. Research on this program reveals that the families who were relocated to housing in the suburbs experienced significantly higher rates of employment, lower school dropout rates, and higher college attendance rates.[55]

Although some believed that the Gautreaux program removed the self-selection bias problem in a quasi-experimental way, "critics were not mollified," because the selection of participants and their placement in new neighborhoods were nonrandom.[56] That is, "the Gautreaux program was the result of a court-ordered desegregation ruling and not a research experiment,"[57] so some argued that self-selection was still a factor. After all, Gautreaux participants were persons struggling to leave poor, inner-city neighborhoods. Some might argue that perhaps they were successful in their new setting not because they were no longer defeated by structural factors, but because they had the gumption to fight their way out of the ghetto in the first place.

These criticisms were addressed in HUD's MTO demonstration program. More specifically, from 1994 to 1997 HUD conducted a lottery that awarded housing vouchers to families living in public housing developments in high-poverty neighborhoods in five cities: Boston, Baltimore, Chicago, Los Angeles, and New York. Families who entered the lottery, thus indicating their desire to move, were randomly assigned to one of three groups. One was awarded housing vouchers that could be used to rent in the private market in any area, one was awarded housing vouchers restricted to private rentals in low-poverty neighborhoods, and one did not receive either of the two vouchers and was therefore treated as a control group to be compared with the other two groups.

The MTO interim evaluation studies were considered superior to the research on the Gautreaux program—as well as other research on neighborhood effects—because they were based on data from a randomized experimental design that eliminated the self-selection bias "that had made it difficult to clearly determine the association between living in poor neighborhoods and individual outcomes."[58] The reports and publications on the interim evaluation, which was finalized in 2003, provided mixed evidence for neighborhood effects in comparisons between the group whose MTO vouchers were restricted to low-poverty areas and the group that did not receive vouchers. On the one hand, during the five-year period following random assignment, the MTO movers who had relocated to low-poverty areas were more likely to have experienced improvements in mental health and less likely to be obese, and girls experienced a significant reduction in "risky behavior" (drinking, taking drugs, engaging in sex, and so on). On the other hand, research investigators found no evidence of an impact on employment rates and earnings, or of any marked improvement on the educational or physical health outcomes of children and young men. These mixed results have led some, including reporters, to question whether there really are enduring negative effects of living in poor, segregated neighborhoods.

However, although the research on the MTO experiment is rigorous, serious problems with the design of the experiment limit the extent to which one can generalize about neighborhood effects. First of all, the treatment was weak. That is, the voucher was restricted for only one year, and the restrictions were based on neighborhood poverty, not racial composition. Indeed, many MTO movers relocated to neighborhoods that were not significantly different from the ones they had left. For example, three-fifths of MTO families entered highly segregated black neighborhoods. Such neighborhoods tend to be considerably less advantaged than integrated areas. Sociologist Robert Sampson analyzed the neighborhood attainment of all Chicago MTO families and found that after approximately seven years, although the voucher winners resided in neighborhoods with poverty rates somewhat lower than in the neighborhoods of control families, both groups had clustered in segregated black neighborhoods that were still considerably poorer than what an overwhelming majority of Americans will ever experience (neighborhoods with poverty rates of roughly 30 percent).[59]

One of the major differences between Gautreaux and MTO was that many Gautreaux families with vouchers moved to *white* suburban areas that were *significantly less impoverished* than their previous neighborhoods. In addition, at the time of the experiment's interim evaluation, as many as 41 percent of the MTO families who had entered low-poverty neighborhoods subsequently moved back to more disadvantaged neighborhoods. Because of such extensive out-migration, these MTO families accumulated relatively little time in areas of low poverty, and correspondingly they did not have an extended opportunity to experience life in low-poverty neighborhoods that were racially integrated.[60]

Moreover, nearly three-fourths of the children in the MTO experiment remained in the same school district, often in the same schools, at the time of the interim evaluation. Stefanie Deluca's comment on these findings, based on her interviews of MTO parents in Baltimore, reveals that school choice was a low priority for some parents. "It is quite striking," she states, "how little some parents thought that school mattered for learning, relative to what the child contributed through hard work and a 'good attitude.'"[61] Furthermore, as pointed out by Quigley and Raphael, the experiment had not improved accessibility to employment opportunities for MTO movers, because their new neighborhoods were no closer to areas of employment growth.[62] Finally, a number of the projects that had housed many participants prior to their MTO relocation were torn down during the time of the experiment, forcing individuals in the control groups to also move and thus making it difficult to determine differences between voucher families and those without vouchers.

Rather than concluding from this research that neighborhoods do not matter, it would be prudent to state simply that although the MTO research raises questions about the extent to which neighborhoods affect the social outcomes of children and adults, it certainly does not resolve these questions. The MTO is best viewed as a policy experiment rather than a measure of social processes. We learn a lot from the MTO regarding how helpful it would be to offer ghetto residents housing vouchers with restricted use based on neighborhood poverty for one year. What the MTO tells us little about is the effect of neighborhoods on the development of children and families.

I think that overall quantitative studies generate mixed or weak findings about the effects of living in poor, segregated neighborhoods because of crude or inadequate measures to capture neighborhood effects. If a random experiment or even a non-experimental study could be generated that would allow researchers to capture the impact of a range of factors distinguishing different neighborhoods, including identifying factors that are cumulative over time, there would be significantly different findings on the impact of living in inner-city ghetto neighborhoods. Allow me to elaborate briefly.

In an impressive study that analyzes data from the Panel Study of Income Dynamics (PSID), a national longitudinal survey, with methods designed to measure intergenerational economic mobility, Patrick Sharkey found that "more than 70% of black children who are raised in the poorest quarter of American neighborhoods will continue to live in the poorest quarter of neighborhoods as adults."[63] He also found that since the 1970s, a majority of black families have resided in the poorest quarter of neighborhoods in *consecutive generations*, compared to only 7 percent of white families. Thus, he concludes that the disadvantages of living in poor, black neighborhoods, like the advantages of living in affluent, white neighborhoods, are in large measure inherited.

Accordingly, this persistence of neighborhood inequality raises serious questions about studies on neighborhood effects. Many of these studies substantially underestimate the racial inequality in neighborhood environments because they use a single-point-in-time, or a single-generation, measure of neighborhood poverty or income.[64] Whereas living in the most impoverished neighborhoods is a temporary state for white families, most black families who lived in the poorest neighborhoods in the 1970s continue to live in such neighborhoods today. Sharkey suggests, therefore, that the focus of the research on neighborhood effects might be shifted to an examination of how the effect of living in poor neighborhoods over two or more generations differs from the effect of short-term residence in such neighborhoods. This brings us back to another shortcoming of the MTO experiment. Sharkey states the following:

> The difficulty with interpreting the results from the MTO as estimates of "neighborhood effects" lies in the conceptualization of a move to a new neighborhood as a point-in-time "treatment." This perspective ignores the possibility that the social environments surrounding families over generations have any lagged or cumulative influence on family members, and it ignores the complex pathways by which this influence may occur. For instance, the neighborhood may have an influence on an individual's educational attainment in one generation, in turn influencing the individual's occupational status and income as an adult, the quality of the home environment in which that individual raises a child, and the developmental trajectory of that child. These indirect pathways are obscured in observational studies that control for a set of covariates such as education or the quality of the home environment, and they are impossible to assess in experimental approaches such as MTO.[65]

We should also consider another pathbreaking study that Sharkey coauthored with senior investigator Robert Sampson and another colleague, Steven Raudenbush, that examined the durable effects of concentrated poverty on black children's verbal ability.[66] They studied a representative sample of 750 African American children, ages six to twelve, who were growing up in the city of

Chicago in 1995, and followed them anywhere they moved in the United States for up to seven years. The children were given a reading examination and vocabulary test at three different periods. The study shows "that residing in a severely disadvantaged neighborhood cumulatively impedes the development of academically relevant verbal ability in children"—so much so that the effects linger even if the children leave these neighborhoods.[67]

The results of this study reveal (1) that the neighborhood environment "is an important developmental context for trajectories of verbal cognitive ability";[68] (2) that young African American children who had earlier lived in a severely disadvantaged neighborhood had fallen behind their counterparts or peers who had not resided previously in disadvantaged areas by up to 6 "IQ" points—a magnitude estimated to be equivalent to "missing a year or more of schooling";[69] and (3) "that the strongest effects appear several years after children live in areas of concentrated disadvantage."[70] This research raises important questions "about ways in which neighborhoods may alter growth in verbal ability producing effects that linger on even if a child leaves a severely disadvantaged neighborhood."[71] Sampson, Sharkey, and Raudenbush argue that if researchers were trying to determine the extent to which neighborhoods affect children's verbal ability by randomly providing housing vouchers to black children who live and grew up in inner-city ghetto neighborhoods and who took a test measuring verbal ability before they moved, and then compared the results of the same test a few years later after the children had resided in better neighborhoods, the conclusion would very likely be that there are no neighborhood effects. Why? Because there would be no difference in verbal ability linked to movement to a better neighborhood, since verbal abilities would have already been formed.

The notion that the children's verbal ability was not affected by their early years in a disadvantaged neighborhood would be quite misleading, they point out, because it does not take into account the significant lagged effect of living in neighborhoods of concentrated disadvantage—effects that linger even after environmental conditions improve. Accordingly, they remarked, "It follows that residential mobility programs for those who grow up in poverty do not necessarily provide the appropriate test of the causal effect of neighborhood social contexts."[72] In other words, the lack of evidence for neighborhood effects in the MTO evaluation does not necessarily suggest the absence of cumulative or durable neighborhood effects.

The studies by Sharkey and by Sampson and his colleagues both suggest that neighborhood effects are not solely structural. Among the effects of living in segregated neighborhoods over extended periods is repeated exposure to cultural traits (including linguistic patterns, the focus of Sampson's study) that emanate from or are the products of racial exclusion—traits, such as poor verbal skills, that may impede successful maneuvering in the larger society.

As Sharkey points out, "when we consider that the vast majority of black families living in America's poorest neighborhoods come from families that have lived in similar environments for generations . . . continuity of the neighborhood environment, in addition to continuity of individual economic status, may be especially relevant to the study of cultural patterns and social norms among disadvantaged populations."[73]

Unfortunately, very little research has focused on these cumulative cultural experiences, and it is sometimes difficult to separate cumulative cultural experiences from cumulative psychological experiences. Take, for example, the repeated experiences of discrimination and disrespect that a lot of blacks have in common. As University of Wisconsin sociologist Erik Olin Wright points out, if these experiences are systematic over an extended time period, they can generate common psychological states that may be erroneously interpreted as norms by social investigators because they seem to regulate patterns of behavior.[74] Resignation as a response to repeated experiences with discrimination and disrespect is one good example. Parents in segregated communities who have had such experiences may transmit to children, through the process of socialization, a set of beliefs about what to expect from life and how one should respond to life circumstances. In other words, children may be taught norms of resignation—they observe the behavior of adults and learn the "appropriate" action or response in different situations independently of their own direct experiences. In the process, children may acquire a disposition to interpret the way the world works that reflects a strong sense that other members of society disrespect them because they are black.

The impact of chronic economic subordination and displays of disrespect on people's psychological dispositions and emotional states may depend partly on the cultural resources they have to interpret what has happened to them, such as a cultural framing designed to fend off insults that promotes strong feelings of racial pride within the community. Over time, "the shared psychological dispositions can become crystallized in cultural products and practices."[75]

Thus, in addition to structural influences, exposure to different cultural influences in the neighborhood environment over time must be taken into account if one is to really appreciate and explain the divergent social outcomes of human groups. But, to repeat, in delivering this message we must make sure that the powerful influence of structural factors does not recede into the background.

Structure versus Culture

In addition to making sure that the structural effects of living in poor neighborhoods are not dismissed or treated lightly, it is important to be clear that structural factors are likely to play a far greater role than cultural factors in bringing about rapid neighborhood change. Persuasive structural evidence for this argument is provided in two studies by University of Texas social scientist Paul Jargowsky. First, in *Poverty and Place*, an important book published by the Russell Sage Foundation in 1997, Jargowsky reveals that in metropolitan areas around the country, changes in economic activity were related to both rapid increases and decreases in neighborhood poverty. Economic booms sharply decreased ghetto poverty in the Southwest in the 1970s and in the Northeast in the 1980s. A rise in the overall mean income resulted in sharp declines in ghetto poverty concentration among blacks.

As Jargowsky correctly observes, "a self-sustaining neighborhood culture implies that levels of neighborhood poverty would respond slowly, if at all, to increased economic opportunity."[76] However, this assumption is undermined not only in his book *Poverty and Place*. A later report that Jargowsky prepared for the Brookings Institution revealed that the number of people residing in high-poverty neighborhoods decreased by 24 percent, or 2.5 million people, from 1990 to 2000 because of the economic boom, particularly in the last half of the 1990s. Moreover, the number of such neighborhoods around the country—the study defined them as census tracts with at least 40 percent of residents below the poverty level—declined by more than a quarter.[77]

In 1990 almost a third of all American blacks lived in such neighborhoods; the 2000 figure was 19 percent. Yet despite this significant improvement, African Americans still have the highest rates of concentrated poverty of all groups in the United States. In part, the state of inner-city ghettos is a legacy of historic racial subjugation. Concentrated-poverty neighborhoods are the most visible and disturbing displays of racial and income segregation. And the dramatic decline in concentrated poverty from 1990 to 2000 can be explained in terms of culture. Rather, these shifts demonstrate that the fate of African Americans and other racial groups is inextricably connected with changes across the modern economy.

Jargowsky's data bear this out. The declines in concentrated poverty in the 1990s occurred not just in a few cities but across the country. By contrast, Los Angeles and Washington DC were two of the few central cities that experienced a rise in concentrated poverty during the 1990s. Jargowsky advances three arguments to account for the divergent trend in Los Angeles: (1) the Rodney King verdict in 1992 triggered a very destructive riot; (2) the number of Latinos immigrating from Mexico and other Central and South American countries into high-poverty neighborhoods was significant; and (3) "the recession in the early 1990s was particularly severe in Southern California, and the economic recovery there was not as rapid as in other parts of California."[78]

In Washington DC the devastating fiscal crisis from the early to the mid-1990s resulted in drastic reductions in public services and an erosion of public confidence in the district's government. This development contributed to "a rapid out-migration of moderate- and middle-income black families, particularly into suburban Maryland counties to the east of the central city. The poor were left behind in economically isolated neighborhoods with increasing poverty rates."[79]

Virtually all racial and ethnic groups recorded improvements. The number of whites living in high-poverty neighborhoods declined by 29 percent (from 2.7 million people to 1.9 million), and the number of blacks decreased by 36 percent (from 4.8 million to 3.1 million). Latinos were the major exception to this pattern because their numbers in high-poverty areas increased slightly during the 1990s, by 1.6 percent. However, this finding should be placed in the context of Latino population growth: the number of Latinos overall increased dramatically in the 1990s, by 57.9 percent, compared with 16.2 percent growth for African Americans and only 3.4 percent for whites.[80] Particularly low-skilled immigrants drove Latino population growth. For all races, the greatest improvements against poverty concentration were in the South and Midwest, and the smallest were in the Northeast, mirroring wider economic trends.[81]

Thus, the notable reduction in the number of high-poverty neighborhoods and the substantial decrease in the population of such neighborhoods may simply be blips of economic booms rather than permanent trends. Unemployment and individual poverty rates have increased since 2000, and we have every reason to assume that concentrated poverty rates are on the rise again as well, although complete data on concentrated poverty for this period will become available only in the 2010 census.

The earlier increase in concentrated poverty occurred during a period of rising income inequality for all Americans that began in the early 1970s. This was a period of decline in inflation-adjusted average incomes among the poor and of growing economic segregation caused by the exodus of middle-income families from inner cities. What had been mixed-income neighborhoods were rapidly transformed into areas of high poverty. Undoubtedly, if the robust economy of the latter 1990s could have been extended for several more years rather than coming to an abrupt halt in 2001, concentrated poverty in inner cities would have declined even more. Here, once again, we see the importance and power of structural forces—in this case, impersonal economic forces—on significantly changing concentrated poverty.

Conclusion

In this chapter I discussed a number of structural forces that have adversely affected inner-city black neighborhoods. These forces included political actions that were explicitly racial, those that were at least partly influenced by race, and those that were ostensibly nonracial (but nevertheless adversely affected black neighborhoods), as well as impersonal economic forces that accelerated neighborhood decline in the inner city and increased disparities in race and income between cities and suburbs.

One of the combined effects of these factors was the emergence of depopulated ghettos, especially in cities of the Midwest and Northeast. Federal transportation and highway policy, along with mortgage-interest tax exemptions, facilitated the exodus of both industries and nonpoor families from inner-city neighborhoods. In turn, the decline of industrial employment in the inner city brought about the end of the Second Great Migration from the South to the North around 1970. These developments helped transform many poor African American neighborhoods, especially those in the Northeast and Midwest, from densely packed areas of recently arrived migrants from the South to neighborhoods gradually abandoned by the working and middle classes.

A number of studies have raised questions about the real effects of living in these ghetto neighborhoods, including the widely cited studies on the Moving to Opportunity (MTO) experiment. In this chapter I highlighted two pathbreaking studies that raise serious questions about the extent to which the MTO captured the effects of living in poor neighborhoods. These two important studies provide compelling evidence for considering the cumulative and often durable effects of residing in poor, segregated neighborhoods. They also provide direction for much-needed research on the cumulative effects of living in poor, segregated neighborhoods. Some of these effects are obviously structural (e.g., proximity to jobs and enrollment in low-quality schools), but others are cultural, such as prolonged exposure to cultural traits that originate from or are the products of racial exclusion (e.g., the development of language skills and the influence of norms of resignation in response to repeated experiences of discrimination and disrespect).

Finally, as shown in this chapter, if one attempts to explain rapid changes in social and economic outcomes, there is little evidence that cultural forces carry the power of structural forces. We need only consider the impact of the economic boom on the reduction of concentrated racial poverty in the 1990s, as discussed in this chapter, for illustration of this point. Although cultural forces play a role in inner-city outcomes, evidence suggests that they are secondary to the larger economic and political forces, both racial and nonracial, that move American society. Indeed, as I will attempt to demonstrate in the next two chapters, structural conditions provide the context within which cultural responses to chronic economic and racial subordination are developed.

CHAPTER 3

THE ECONOMIC PLIGHT OF INNER-CITY BLACK MALES

The economic predicament of low-skilled black men in the inner city has reached catastrophic proportions. Americans may not fully understand the dreadful social and economic circumstances that have moved these black males further and further behind the rest of society, but they often fear black males and perceive that they pose a problem for those who live in the city. Elliot Liebow helped expand our understanding of low-skilled black males when he wrote *Tally's Corner: A Study of Street Corner Men* in the mid-1960s.[1] Since then, researchers have paid more attention to this group.

Although many of Liebow's arguments concerning the work experiences and family lives of black men in a Washington DC ghetto are still applicable to contemporary urban communities, the social and economic predicament of low-skilled black males today, especially their rate of joblessness, has become even more severe. Liebow was perhaps the first scholar to demonstrate that an ongoing lack of success in the labor market (ranging from outright unemployment to being trapped in menial jobs) leads to a lessening of self-confidence and, eventually, to feelings of resignation that frequently result in temporary, or even permanent, abandonment of looking for work.

Even when Liebow's men were successful in finding work, the jobs they occupied paid little and were dirty, physically demanding, and uninteresting. This work did not foster respect, build status, or offer opportunity for advancement. "The most important fact [in becoming discouraged from looking for or keeping a job] is that a man who is able and willing to work cannot earn enough to support himself, his wife, and one or more children," declared Liebow. "A man's chances for working regularly are good only if he is willing to work for less than he can live on, sometimes not even then."[2] Because they held the same ideas about work and reward as other Americans, the street-corner men viewed such jobs disdainfully. "He cannot do otherwise," stated Liebow. "He cannot draw from a job those values which other people do not put into it."[3] Unlike today, menial employment was readily available to these men during the 1960s, and they drifted from one undesirable job to the next.

When I analyzed the data collected from the mid-1980s to the mid-1990s by our research team on poverty and joblessness among black males in inner-city Chicago neighborhoods,[4] I was repeatedly reminded of Liebow's book. Although the job prospects for low-skilled black men were bleak when Liebow conducted his field research in the early 1960s, they were even worse in the last quarter of the twentieth century, when even menial jobs in the service sector were difficult for low-skilled black males to find. That situation persists today. Indeed, the employment woes of poor black men represent part of "the new urban poverty," which I define as poor, segregated neighborhoods in which substantial proportions of the adult population are either officially unemployed or have dropped out of, or never entered, the labor force. This jobless poverty today stands in sharp contrast to previous periods, when the working poor predominated in urban ghettos.[5] For example, in Chicago's Bronzeville neighborhoods—Douglas, Grand Boulevard, and Washington Park, the traditional black-belt area where the original black migrants from the South settled in the early twentieth century on Chicago's South Side—64 percent of all males fourteen years and older held jobs in a typical week in 1960. By 1990, a few years before Douglas and Grand Boulevard experienced gentrification, only 37 percent of all males sixteen and over worked in a typical week.[6]

A recent article by Allison K. Rodean and Christopher H. Wheeler provides data on changes in the clustering of unemployment in urban neighborhoods across the nation. Rodean and Wheeler state,

> Based on data from the decennial U.S. Census covering more than 165,000 block groups located in 361 metropolitan areas, neighborhoods increasingly divided into high- and low-unemployment areas between 1980 and 2000. Rates of unemployment tended to fall in neighborhoods that already had low rates of unemployment in 1980, while they tended to rise in neighborhoods that had relatively high rates of unemployment in 1980. People without a job therefore, were more likely to come from one of a handful of high-unemployment neighborhoods in 2000 than two decades earlier."[7]

As the authors point out, neighborhoods with larger fractions of nonwhites tend to be associated with higher rates of unemployment. Note, however, that the Rodean and Wheeler study high-lights only *unemployment* in poor neighborhoods. When I speak of "joblessness," I am not referring solely to unemployment as it is officially measured. In the United States, the unemployment rate takes into account only those workers who are currently in the official labor force—that is, those who are *actively* looking for work (according to monthly interviews of a representative sample of households in the United States by the US Bureau of Labor Statistics). I use the term *joblessness*, then, to refer not only to those who are actively looking for work, but also to those who remain outside of or who have dropped out of the labor market. In early 2008, for example, although the official unemployment rate among men of ages twenty-five to fifty-four was 4.1 percent, the jobless rate was 13.1 percent.[8] This larger number includes millions of adult males who are not recorded in official US labor market statistics, either because they are not looking for a job or because they are incarcerated. And they tend to disproportionately reside in poor, inner-city neighborhoods.

In the last four decades, low-skilled African American males have encountered increasing difficulty gaining access to jobs—even menial jobs paying no more than the minimum wage. The ranks of idle inner-city men have swelled since 1970, and they include a growing proportion of unemployed adult males who routinely work in and tolerate low-wage jobs when they are available.[9]

The impact of this joblessness is reflected in real earnings (earnings adjusted for inflation). For example, between 2000 and 2004 the average real annual earnings of twenty-four-year-old black males who were in the bottom quarter of the earnings distribution (i.e., the 25th percentile of earnings) were only $1,078, compared with $9,623 for Latino males and $9,843 for white males in the bottom quarter of their earnings distributions.[10] Although the earnings of Latino and white males at the 25th percentile were also relatively low, they were nine times higher than those of comparable black males. The extremely limited average annual earnings for black males at the low end of the earnings distribution reflect their significantly higher jobless rates during this period, including those who had completely given up looking for work and had virtually no reported income. For purposes of comparison, if we move to the 75th percentile of the earnings distribution, the average annual earnings for twenty-four-year-old black males during this period were $22,000, compared with earnings of $22,800 and $30,000 for Latino and white males, respectively. These numbers illustrate that the really significant discrepancy in work and wages is for those in the bottom quartile—the poorest men.

A closer look reveals that many of these jobless men are high school dropouts whose situations are especially bleak. A recent report by Andrew Sum and his colleagues at Northeastern University's Center for Labor Market Studies revealed that "only 1 of every 3 young black male high school dropouts was able to obtain any type of employment during an average month in 2005," and only 23 percent of such males were able to find full-time employment during an average week.[11] The report appropriately points out that "many of these young men will end up being involved in criminal activity during their late teens and early 20s and then bear the severe economic consequences for convictions and incarceration over the remainder of their working lives."[12]

The declining relative status of black males is not restricted to poor, low-skilled workers. Indeed, black women have far outpaced black men in college completion in recent years. Across all racial groups there has been an overall growing gender gap in college degree attainment, with women generally exceeding men in rates of college completion. However, this discrepancy is particularly acute among African Americans, and the gap has widened steadily in the past twenty-five years. In 1979, for every 100 bachelor's degrees earned by black men, 144 were earned by black women. In 2003–2004, for every 100 bachelor's degrees conferred on black men, 200 were conferred on black women. To put this gap into a larger context, for every 100 bachelor's degrees earned by white men and Hispanic men, white women earned 155 and Hispanic women 131 degrees.[13]

The ever-increasing discrepancy in the college graduation rates of black men and black women is significant because the economic rewards of a college education are particularly high for black males. Figure 3.1, which provides data on the employment-to-population ratio—the percentage of young men who were not in school and who were employed—in 2005, reveals that there is very little difference in the employment rates of black, white, and

Figure 3.1

Employment-to-Population Ratios of Nonenrolled Sixteen- to Twenty-Four-Year-Old Males by Educational Attainment and Racial/Ethnic Group in the United States, 2005

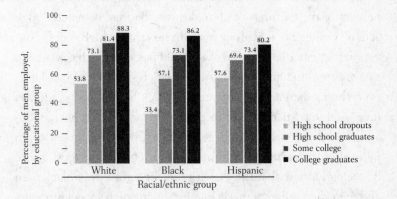

Adapted from Andrew Sum, Ishwar Khatiwada, Joseph McLaughlin, and Paulo Tobar, "The Educational Attainment of the Nation's Young Black Men and Their Recent Labor Market Experiences: What Can be Done to Improve Their Future Labor Market and Educational Prospects?" (paper prepared for Jobs for America's Graduates, Alexandria, VA, February 2007).

Hispanic college graduates. The rate is 88.3 percent for whites, 86.2 for blacks, and 80.2 for Hispanics—a range of less than 10 percentage points across all three groups. However, the employment gap widens dramatically when we consider persons with lower levels of education. The employment gap between white young men and black young men ages sixteen to twenty-four who were not in school in 2005 was 20 percentage points for high school dropouts, 16 among high school graduates, 8 for those completing one to three years of college, and, as we saw in the earlier example, only 2 for four-year college graduates. These data show that education plays a key role in enabling black men to secure employment.

Similar to the findings on employment rates for young men out of school, Figure 3.2 shows that the relative gap in annual earnings between twenty- and twenty-nine-year-old black men and men in the same age group of all racial/ethnic groups decreases at higher levels of education. The median annual earnings of black males with less than a high school education were equivalent to only 15 percent of the earnings of all males who had not completed high school. For instance, if all males with less than a high school education had a median income of $20,000 per year, the black men in this group would have a median income of $3,000 per year. However, the median annual earnings of black high school graduates increased to 64 percent of those earned by all high school graduates, and those of black college graduates were equivalent to 96 percent of the earnings of all men with bachelor's degrees. These data clearly show that the disparity in the earnings of black men and men from other groups is highest among high school dropouts and almost vanishes among college graduates.

The deteriorating economic plight of inner-city, low-skilled black males reduces the relative size of the pool of potential candidates in poorer black communities who can climb the educational

Figure 3.2

Ratio of the Median Annual Earnings of Twenty- to Twenty-Nine-Year-Old Black Men to All Men by Educational Attainment, 2004–2005

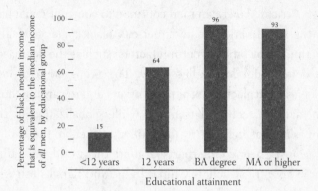

Adapted from Andrew Sum, Ishwar Khatiwada, Joseph McLaughlin, and Paulo Tobar, "The Educational Attainment of the Nation's Young Black Men and Their Recent Labor Market Experiences: What Can be Done to Improve Their Future Labor Market and Educational Prospects?" (paper prepared for Jobs for America's Graduates, Alexandria, VA, February 2007).

ladder and ultimately obtain a college education. Although we lack conclusive evidence, it is reasonable to assume that the growing gap in the college graduation rates of black females and black males stems in part from the socioeconomic woes of those young African American males who are positioned at the bottom of the American occupational structure and who face more obstacles to advancement, including enrollment in college. These obstacles, which arise from both structural and cultural causes, are the focus of this chapter.

The Role of Structural Factors

Although African American men continue to confront racial barriers in the labor market, many inner-city black males have also
been victimized by other structural factors, such as the decreased
relative demand for low-skilled labor. The propagation of new
technologies is displacing untrained workers and rewarding those
with specialized, technical training, while globalization of the
economy is increasingly pitting low-skilled workers in the United
States against their counterparts around the world, including
laborers in countries such as China, India, and Bangladesh who
can be employed for substantially lower wages. This decreasing
relative demand in the United States for low-skilled labor means
that untrained workers face the growing threat of eroding wages
and job displacement.[14]

Over the past several decades, African Americans have experienced sharp job losses in the manufacturing sector. Indeed, as
John Schmitt and Ben Zipperer point out, "the share of black workers in manufacturing has actually been falling more rapidly than
the overall share of manufacturing employment. From the end
of the 1970s through the early 1990s, African Americans were
just as likely as workers from other racial and ethnic groups to
have manufacturing jobs. Since the early 1990s, however, black
workers have lost considerable ground in manufacturing. By 2007,
blacks were about 15 percent less likely than other workers to have
a job in manufacturing."[15] The dwindling proportion of African
American workers in manufacturing is important because manufacturing jobs, especially those in the auto industry, have been a
significant source of better-paid employment for black Americans
since World War II.[16]

The relative decline of black workers in manufacturing parallels their decreasing involvement in unions. From 1983 to 2007 the proportion of all African American workers who were either in unions or represented by a union at their employment site dropped considerably, from 31.7 to 15.7 percent. In 2007, African American workers were still more likely to be unionized (15.7 percent) than whites (13.5) and Hispanics (10.8). Nonetheless, this reduction (down 16 percentage points) over that time span was greater than that for whites (down 8.9 percentage points) and Hispanics (down 13.4).[17] The lack of union representation renders workers more vulnerable in the workplace, especially to cuts in wages and benefits.

Because they tend to be educated in poorly performing public schools, low-skilled black males often enter the job market lacking some of the basic tools that would help them confront changes in their employment prospects. Such schools have rigid district bureaucracies, poor morale among teachers and school principals, low expectations for students, and negative ideologies that justify poor student performance. Inner-city schools fall well below more advantaged suburban schools in science and math resources, and they lack teachers with appropriate preparation in these subjects.[18] As a result, students from these schools tend to have poor reading and math skills, important tools for competing in the globalized labor market. Few thoughtful observers of public education would disagree with the view that the poor employment prospects of low-skilled black males are in no small measure related to their public-education experiences.

Their lack of education, which contributes to joblessness, is certainly related to their risk of incarceration. As Bruce Western so brilliantly revealed in his important book *Punishment and Inequality in America*, following the collapse of the low-skilled urban labor markets and the creation of jobless ghettos in our nation's inner cities, incarceration grew among those with the highest rates of joblessness.[19] "By the early 2000s," states West-ern, "the chances of imprisonment were more closely linked to race and school failure than at any time in the previous twenty years."[20] Between 1979 and 1999, the risk of imprisonment for less educated men nearly doubled. Indeed, a significant proportion of black men who have been in prison are high school dropouts. "Among [black] male high school dropouts the risk of imprison-ment [has] increased to 60 percent, establishing incarceration as a normal stopping point on the route to midlife."[21]

However, Western's research also revealed that national cul-tural shifts in values and attitudes contributed to a political con-text associated with a resurgent Republican Party that focused on punitive "solutions" and worsened the plight of low-skilled black men. This more penal approach to crime was reinforced during Bill Clinton's administration. Indeed, rates of incarceration soared even during periods when the overall crime rate had declined. "The growth in violence among the ghetto poor through the 1960s and 1970s stoked fears of white voters and lurked in the rhetoric of law and order," states Western. "Crime, however, did not drive the rise in imprisonment directly, but formed the background for a new style of politics and punishment. As joblessness and low wages became enduring features of the less skilled inner-city economy, the effects of a punitive criminal justice system concentrated on the most disadvantaged."[22] Western estimates that as many as 30 percent of all civilian young adult black males ages sixteen to thirty-four are ex-offenders.[23] In short, cultural shifts in attitudes toward crime and punishment created struc-tural circumstances—a more punitive criminal justice system—that have had a powerful impact on low-skilled black males.

Finally, as Harry Holzer and his colleagues remind us, the high amount of child support now required of noncustodial fathers under federal law presents a daunting problem and aggravates the employment woes of low-skilled black males. Such payments can represent an employment tax of 36 percent of a worker's wages, and if the noncustodial father is in arrears, the federal law allows states to deduct as much as 65 percent of his wages. Many of those who face this higher tax are ex-offenders whose delinquent child support payments accumulated while they were in prison. For many low-skilled black males, high child support payments are a disincentive to remain in the formal labor market and an incentive to move into the casual or informal labor market.[24]

This is certainly not to suggest that if these men were relieved of the high child support payments they would be more likely to make predictable and routine support payments to the mothers of their children, even if they derived income from the underground economy (i.e., including income from jobs in the informal labor market that skirt federal pay regulations and pay their employees "under the table"). It is also not to suggest that fathers should not provide financial support to their children. Rather, the potential of high child support payments can be added to the list of structural factors that contribute to the joblessness of poor black men as officially defined.

For inner-city black male workers, the problems created by these structural factors have been aggravated by employers' negative attitudes toward black men as workers. A representative sample of Chicago-area employers by my research team in the late 1980s clearly reveals employer bias against black males.[25] A substantial majority of employers considered inner-city black males to be uneducated, uncooperative, unstable, or dishonest.[26] For example, a suburban drug store manager made the following comment:

> It's unfortunate but, in my business I think overall [black men] tend to be known to be dishonest. I think that's too bad but that's the image they have. (*Interviewer*: So you think it's an image

problem?) *Respondent*: An image problem of being dishonest men and lazy. They're known to be lazy. They are [laughs]. I hate to tell you, but. It's all an image though. Whether they are or not, I don't know, but, it's an image that is perceived, (*Interviewer*: I see. How do you think that image was developed?) *Respondent*: Go look in the jails [laughs].

The president of an inner-city manufacturing firm expressed a different reservation about employing black males from certain ghetto neighborhoods:

If somebody gave me their address, uh, Cabrini Green I might unavoidably have some concerns. (*Interviewer*: What would your concerns be?) *Respondent*: That the poor guy probably would be frequently unable to get to work and . . . I probably would watch him more carefully even if it wasn't fair, than I would with somebody else. I know what I should do though is recognize that here's a guy that is trying to get out of his situation and probably will work harder than somebody else who's already out of there and he might be the best one around here. But I think I would have to struggle accepting that premise at the beginning.

The prevalence of such attitudes, combined with the physical and social isolation of minorities living in inner-city areas of concentrated poverty, severely limits the access that poor black men have to informal job networks (the casual networks of people or acquaintances who can pass along information about employment prospects). This is a notable problem for black males, especially considering that many low-skilled employees first learn about their jobs through an acquaintance or were recommended by someone associated with the company. Research suggests that only a small percentage of low-skilled employees are hired through advertised

job openings or cold calls.[27] The importance of knowing someone
who knows the boss can be seen by another employer's comments
to our interviewer:

> All of a sudden, they take a look at a guy, and unless he's got an
> in, the reason why I hired this black kid the last time is cause
> my neighbor said to me, yeah I used him for a few [days], he's
> good, and I said, you know what, I'm going to take a chance. But
> it was a recommendation. But other than that, I've got a walk-in,
> and, who knows? And I think that for the most part, a guy sees
> a black man, he's a bit hesitant.

These attitudes are classic examples of what social scientists
call statistical discrimination: employers make generalizations
about inner-city, black male workers and reach decisions based on
those assumptions without reviewing the qualifications of an individual applicant. The net effect is that many inner-city, black male
applicants are never given the opportunity to prove themselves.
Although some of these men scorn entry-level jobs because of the
poor working conditions and low wages, many others would readily
accept such employment. And although statistical discrimination
contains some elements of class bias against poor, inner-city workers, it is clearly a racially motivated practice. It is a frustrating and
disturbing fact that inner-city black males are effectively screened
out of employment far more often than their Hispanic or white
peers who apply for the same jobs. A number of other studies
have documented employer bias against black males. For example,
research by Devah Pager revealed that a white applicant with a
felony conviction was more likely to receive a callback or job offer
than was a black applicant with a clean record.[28]

Although negative employer attitudes exemplify cultural factors in the broader society that adversely affect blacks, I chose to

discuss these attitudes in this section on the impact of structural factors because the cultural framework of employers is definitely related to patterns of employer discrimination—a structural factor. As Erik Olin Wright reminded me, "one person's social structure is another person's culture."[29] As the employers see it, they are expressing not only dominant cultural views about low-skilled black men that are shared by many members of the larger society, but also the shared views of employers regarding their interactions with both immigrant and poor African American workers. As the young black men seeking employment see it, the culturally shaped practice of employers is a "structure"—a pattern of exclusion that is systematically enforced through repeated rejections of their job applications. However, not only do employers share some common cultural beliefs or perceptions about black males, but they also have the power to affect the lives of these black men when they act on those beliefs. Employers make hiring decisions, which is an exercise of power, and their decisions are based on their control over economic resources.

Unfortunately, shifts in the economy from manufacturing to service industries have accompanied changes in the criminal justice system and compounded the negative effects of employers' attitudes toward inner-city black males. Today, most of the new jobs for workers with limited education and experience are in the service sector, which includes jobs that tend to be held by women, such as waitresses, sales clerks, and health care aides. Indeed, "employment rates of young black women now exceed those of young black men, even though many of these women must also care for children."[30]

The shift to service industries has resulted in a greater demand for workers who can effectively serve and relate to the consumer. Many employers in our study favored women and recent immigrants of both genders (who have come to populate the labor pool in the low-wage service sector) over black men for service jobs. Employers in service industries felt that consumers perceived inner-city black males to be dangerous or threatening in part because of their high incarceration rates. In the past, men simply had to demonstrate a strong back and muscles to be hired for physical labor in a factory, at a construction site, or on an assembly line; they interacted with peers and foremen, not with consumers. Today, they have to search for work in the service sector, where employers are less likely to hire them because they are seen as unable to sustain positive contact with the public. Employers in the study maintained that black males lack the soft skills that their jobs require: the tendency to maintain eye contact, the ability to carry on polite and friendly conversations with consumers, the inclination to smile and be responsive to consumer requests no matter how demanding or unreasonable they may seem. Consequently, black male job seekers face rising rates of rejection.

Employer attitudes favoring Hispanic workers over inner-city black workers have also affected black male participation in temporary-employment agencies, which connect unskilled workers to employers in the construction and restaurant industries. Research on the pattern of temporary-employment agencies in Chicago reveals that they tend to be located in neighborhoods with large Latino populations and that they tend to avoid African American neighborhoods. The researchers, Jamie Peck and Nik Theodore, point out that these "agencies' work allocation systems favor 'reliably contingent' workers who are available every day and whose work attitudes, job capabilities and personal attributes render them acceptable to employers . . . In providing what employers want and *expect*, these temp agencies harden and institutionalize processes of labor segmentation at the point of entry into the job market . . . to the detriment of African-American workers."[31]

The high incarceration rates of low-skilled black males are very much connected to their high jobless rates. It is a vicious cycle. Being without a job can encourage illegal moneymaking activities in order to make ends meet, which increases the risks of incarceration. Upon release from incarceration, a prison record carries a stigma in the eyes of employers and decreases the probability that an ex-offender will be hired, resulting in a greater likelihood of even more intractable joblessness.[32]

Forced to turn to the low-wage service sector for employment, inner-city black males—including a significant number of ex-offenders—have to compete, often unsuccessfully, with a growing number of female and immigrant workers. If these men complain or otherwise manifest their dissatisfaction, they seem even more unattractive to employers and therefore encounter even greater discrimination when they search for employment. Because the feelings that many inner-city black males express about their jobs and job prospects reflect their plummeting position in a changing economy, it is important to link these attitudes and other cultural traits with the opportunity structure—that is, the spectrum of life chances available to them in society at large.[33]

Many people would agree that both the structural factors and the national cultural factors discussed earlier have had a very large impact on the experiences of low-skilled black males.[34] But no such consensus exists with respect to the role of cultural factors that have emerged in inner-city ghetto neighborhoods in shaping and directing the lives of young black men.

The Role of Cultural Factors

Throughout this discussion I have suggested that cultural factors must be brought to bear if we are to explain economic and social outcomes for racial groups. The exploration of the cultural dimension must do three things: (1) provide a compelling reason for including cultural factors in a comprehensive discussion of race and poverty, (2) show the relationship between cultural analysis and structural analysis, and (3) determine the extent to which cultural factors operate independently to contribute to or reinforce poverty and racial inequality. However, the evidence for the influence of cultural factors on the social and economic circumstances of low-skilled black males is far less compelling than structural arguments, in part because of a dearth of research in this area.

According to Orlando Patterson of Harvard University, since the mid-1960s a strong bias against cultural explanations for human behavior has led social scientists and policy analysts to ignore different groups' distinctive cultural attributes in favor of an emphasis on structural factors to account for the behavior and social outcomes of its members. So instead of looking at attitudes, norms, values, habits, and worldviews (all indications of cultural orientations), we focus on joblessness, low socioeconomic status, and underperforming public schools—in short, structural factors.

Patterson revisited the role of culture and raised several questions that might be better addressed when cultural elements are considered in conjunction with structural and historical explanations. Patterson asks, "Why do so many young unemployed black men have children—several of them—which they have no resources or intention to support? And why . . . do they murder each other at nine times the rate of white youths?" And, he adds, why do young black males turn their backs on low-wage jobs that immigrants are happy to fill?[35] Referring to research conducted by UCLA sociologist Roger Waldinger,[36] Patterson states that such jobs enable the chronically unemployed to enter the labor market and obtain basic work skills that they can later use in securing better jobs. But he also notes that those who accepted the low-paying jobs in Waldinger's study were mostly immigrants.

To help answer his own questions about the behavior of young black men in the ghetto, Patterson refers to anecdotal evidence collected several years ago by one of his former students. He states that the student visited her former high school to discover why "almost all the black girls graduated and went to college whereas nearly all the black boys either failed to graduate or did not go on to college."[37] Her distressing finding was that all of the black boys were fully aware of the consequences of failing to graduate from high school and go on to college. (They indignantly exclaimed, "We're not stupid!"). So, Patterson wonders, why were they flunking out?[38] The candid answer that these young men gave to his former student was their preference for what some call the "cool-pose culture" of young black men, which they found too fulfilling to give up.[39] "For these young men, it was almost like a drug, hanging out on the street after school, shopping and dressing sharply, sexual conquests, party drugs, hip-hop music and culture."[40]

Patterson maintains that cool-pose culture blatantly promotes the most anomalous models of behavior in urban, lower-class neighborhoods, featuring gangsta rap, predatory sexuality, and irresponsible fathering. "It is reasonable to conclude," he states, "that among a large number of urban, Afro-American lower-class young men, these models are now fully normative and that men act in accordance with them whenever they can."[41] For example, Patterson argues that black male pride has become increasingly defined in terms of the impregnation of women. However, this trend is not unique to the current generation of young black males, he notes. Several decades ago the sociologist Lee Rainwater uncovered a similar pattern. Not only did a majority of the inner-city, young black male respondents he interviewed state that they were indifferent to the fact that their girlfriends were pregnant, but some even expressed the proud belief that getting a girl pregnant proves you're a man.[42] The fact that Elijah Anderson and others discovered identical models decades later suggests the possibility of a pattern of cultural transmission—that is, the attitudes and behaviors valorizing a kind of "footloose fatherhood" have been passed down to younger generations.[43] A counterargument—one that does not assume cultural transmission—could also be posed: young black men in roughly similar structural positions in different generations developed similar cultural responses.

Patterson argues that a thoughtful cultural explanation of the self-defeating behavior of poor, young black men could not only speak to the immediate relationship of their attitudes, behavior, and undesirable outcomes, but also examine their brutalized past, perhaps over generations, to investigate the origins and changing nature of these views and practices. Patterson maintains that we cannot understand the behavior of young black men without deeply examining their collective past.[44]

I believe that Patterson tends to downplay the importance of immediate socioeconomic factors: if there is indeed a cool-pose culture, it is reasonable to assume that it is partly related to employment failures and disillusionment with the poorly performing public schools and possibly has its roots in the special social circumstances fostered by pre-1960s legal segregation. But I fully concur with Patterson's view that cultural explanations that include historical context should be part of our attempt to fully account for behavior that is so contradictory to mainstream ideas of how work and family should fit into a man's life. I also believe it is exceedingly difficult to determine the relative balance between cultural and structural arguments in explaining the behavior and the social and economic circumstances in which we find poor, young black males.

Nevertheless, it is one thing to acknowledge that cultural fac-

tors ought to be included in our quest for understanding, but quite
another thing to advance cultural explanations that are based on
real evidence. Take, for example, the writings of the conservative
political scientist Lawrence Mead on the black subculture.[45] Mead
boldly asserts that the difficulties blacks experience in the labor
market are due in large measure to subcultures of defeatism and
resistance. He argues that defeatism is expressed whenever blacks
confront difficulties in finding and keeping jobs—for example,
obtaining reliable transportation to and from work. Mead contends that blacks give up in the face of such difficulties and tend
to place blame on their unique circumstances or on the actions
of others in the larger society for their employment woes, including the discrimination of employers. They then sit back, Mead
argues, and wait for others to initiate action that would improve
their situation. Mead contends that this failure to assume personal
responsibility stems from deeply internalized feelings of helpless-
ness rooted in slavery, as a result of a "paradoxical reliance on the
oppressor to undo oppression," and passed on from generation to
generation.[46]

In Mead's effort to dismiss immediate structural factors, however, he provides no empirical evidence that this "defeatism" is
an outgrowth of slavery experiences.[47] Nor does his explanation
account for why joblessness in the inner city today is so much
higher than it was, say, in the 1950s and '60s, when an overwhelming majority of poor black adult males were working. Indeed, if
we look solely at the data gathered by social scientists in the field,
there is not a great deal of evidence for a subculture of defeatism;
on the contrary, we see evidence of black struggles to participate,
through work, in the American dream.

In her ethnographic research—that is, work using evidence
gathered through field observation and through extended, often
repeated, interviews—Katherine Newman reveals that young,

low-wage workers in New York City's Harlem neighborhood not only adhere to mainstream values regarding work, but also tend to accept low-skilled, low-wage, often dead-end jobs.[48] In his impressive study of how young, inner-city black men perceive opportunity and mobility in the United States, Alford Young found that although some men associated social mobility with the economic opportunity structure, including race- and class-based discrimination, all of his respondents shared the view that individuals are largely accountable for their failure to advance in society.[49]

The research conducted by my team in Chicago provides only mixed evidence for a subculture of defeatism. Consistent with Liebow's findings in *Tally's Corner*, the ethnographic research in our study revealed that many young black males had experienced repeated failures in their job search, had given up hope, and therefore no longer bothered to look for work.[50] This discouragement has some parallels with Mead's thesis, but our research pointed to negative employer attitudes and actions toward low-skilled black males as powerful influences in this cycle. Our ethnographic research suggested that repeated failure results in resignation and the development of cultural attitudes that discourage the pursuit of steady employment in the formal labor market.

On the other hand, data from our large, random survey of black residents in the inner city revealed that despite the overwhelming joblessness and poverty around them, black residents in ghetto neighborhoods, consistent with the findings of Alford Young, spoke unambiguously in support of basic American values concerning individual initiative. For example, nearly all of the black people we questioned felt that plain hard work is either very important or somewhat important for getting ahead. In addition, in a series of open-ended interviews conducted by members of our research team, participants overwhelmingly endorsed the dominant American belief system concerning poverty. The views of some of these individuals—who lived in some of the most destitute neighborhoods in America—were particularly revealing. A substantial majority agreed that America is a land of opportunity where anybody can get ahead, and that individuals get pretty much what they deserve.[51]

The response of a thirty-four-year-old black male, a resident in a ghetto area of the South Side of Chicago where 29 percent of the population was destitute (i.e., with incomes 75 percent below the poverty line) was typical: "Everybody get pretty much what they deserve because if everybody wants to do better they got to go out there and try. If they don't try, they won't make it." Another black male who was residing in an equally impoverished South Side neighborhood stated, "For some it's a land of opportunity, but you can't just let opportunity come knock on your door, you just got to go ahead and work for it. You got to go out and get it for yourself." Although their support of this abstract American ideal was not always consistent with their perceptions and descriptions of the social barriers that impeded the social progress of their neighbors and friends, these endorsements stand in strong contrast to the subculture of defeatism that Mead describes. Nonetheless, I should note that there is frequently a gap between what people state in the abstract and what they perceive to be possible for themselves given their own situations. In other words, it should not be surprising if some residents support the abstract American ideal of individual initiative and still feel that they cannot get ahead, because of factors beyond their control.

The inconsistency between what people say in the abstract and what they believe applies to them may be seen in other ways. Jennifer Hochschild's analysis of national survey data reveals that poor blacks tend to acknowledge the importance of discrimination when they respond to national surveys, but they are not likely to feel that it affects them personally.[52] Often, discrimination is the least mentioned factor among other important forces that black people select when asked what determines their chances in life. Thus, among poor blacks, structural factors such as discrimination and declining job opportunities "do not register as major impediments to achieving their goals. Deficient motivation and individual effort do."[53] The emphasis that poor blacks place on the importance of personal attributes over structural factors for success in America should not come as a surprise. As Hochschild astutely points out, "poor African Americans are usually badly educated and not widely traveled, so they are unlikely to see structural patterns underlying individual actions and situations. Thus even if (or because) the American dream fails as a description of American society, it is a highly seductive prescription for succeeding in that society to those who cannot see the underlying flaw."[54] To repeat, the evidence for a subculture of defeatism is mixed. Nonetheless, until more compelling studies are produced, it remains an important hypothesis for research.

In addition to a subculture of defeatism, Mead argues, a subculture of resistance affects black employment outcomes. Like Orlando Patterson—who asserts, on the basis of Roger Waldinger's work, that "black males turn their backs on jobs that immigrants are happy to fill"[55]—Mead argues that the subculture of resistance is not a response to being overwhelmed by the difficulties of obtaining and keeping jobs, but rather an expression of disdain for the jobs—work they feel is too difficult, dirty, demeaning, and poorly paid. And Mead's subculture-of-resistance argument asserts that many African Americans reject low-paying and menial jobs, even though they do not have the qualifications for higher-paying, more satisfying employment. Thus, whereas the subculture of defeatism is a result of having too little pride to succeed in the labor market, the subculture of resistance reflects too much pride to accept menial employment.[56]

Again, neither Patterson nor Mead provides any systematic evidence for a subculture of resistance among the black poor. There is, of course, Patterson's assertion, based on Waldinger's research, that Latino immigrants are more eager workers than inner-city blacks when low-income jobs are available. But Waldinger provides no direct evidence that the black poor in New York reject jobs that immigrants are ready to accept.[57] For his part, Mead simply asserts that poor black youth will not accept menial jobs because, research reveals, they have relatively high standards for what they feel they must be paid before they will accept a job—a concept known as *reservation wages*.[58] As Sandra Smith points out, however, "because Mead does not examine closely and systematically the process of finding work that the black poor undertake, he critically misstates the meanings that the black poor attach to work, job finding, and joblessness."[59] Indeed, argues Smith, "the weight of the evidence indicates that the black poor are not resistant to low-wage work."[60]

If there is insufficient evidence to support the claim that poor blacks tend to reject low-wage work, one careful study suggests that the issue has less to do with a subculture of resistance and more to do with the different cultural frames that immigrants and blacks bring to low-wage jobs. Harvard sociologist Mary Waters' research reveals that West Indian and African American food service workers approach the same menial job with a different mind-set, as reflected in dissimilar attitudes and motivation. For many West Indian immigrants, low-paying jobs are actually seen as "good" jobs, when one considers the wages they would receive in their home countries; whereas African Americans view them as "bad" jobs that remind them of their relatively subordinate socioeconomic position in our society. This does not mean outright rejection of these jobs as Mead asserts, but resentment that they have to accept such work.[61]

Stephen Petterson's research provides the most impressive evidence challenging the subculture-of-resistance thesis.[62] Trained as a sociologist and social statistician, he set out to test assumptions associated with the subculture-of-resistance argument—namely, that low-skilled, young black men are less willing to pursue or accept low-paying jobs because of higher reservation wages (wages that workers are willing to accept for employment), and that their excessive reservation wages result in longer periods of joblessness. Petterson relied on data from the National Longitudinal Survey of Youth (NLSY)—which has been tracking since 1979 a nationally representative sample of more than 12,000 men and women who were between the ages of fourteen and twenty-one on January 1, 1978—to test the subculture-of-resistance thesis. Confining his sample to black men and white men who were not employed, not enrolled in school, and not in jail when interviewed, and who had previous work experience (a total of 2,179 persons), Petterson analyzed annual data on their self-reported reservation wages for jobs that they had sought between 1979 and 1986—the only years such data were collected.

Despite the relative decline in high-paying manufacturing jobs during the 1970s and '80s, argues Petterson, "the 'Great American Machine' has produced millions of jobs. Most, however, offer low wages and little job security."[63] Nonetheless, he adds, the hardcore unemployed may even experience increased difficulty obtaining low-wage jobs, since employers often feel they are unreliable because of their prolonged spells of joblessness. Moreover, the unemployed often compete directly with more highly skilled workers, who themselves end up applying for lesser positions when they experience difficulty finding better jobs. "Indeed," Petterson states, "long queues form even for minimum wage jobs."[64] Once again we see that structural factors play a powerful role in the apportioning of jobs and the benefits that they bring. And Petterson's research does, in fact, show that low-skilled black workers have relatively high reservation wages in comparison with their previous wages, which on the face of things might lead us to conclude that Mead is right to embrace this as a major reason for their joblessness.[65]

Petterson, however, advances an alternative explanation of young, low-skilled black men's relatively high reservation wages, which pertains to the issue of wage fairness. He states, "There may be systematic differences between what job-seekers state in public and what they actually do when confronted with a job offer."[66] He points out that previous research on reservation wages reveals that the reservation wages of job seekers at the bottom of the wage distribution are higher than their previous wages, while the reservation wages of those near the top of the wage distribution are lower than their previous wages.[67] Thus, the fact that reservation wages of poor blacks are higher than their previous wages might be mainly due to their heavy concentration in low-wage jobs and their relatively low starting point—at the lower end of the past-wage distribution.

Petterson's findings lend support to this alternative explanation. He compared the sample of unemployed workers' previous wages with their reservation wages and found that blacks sought wages 16 percent higher than their previous wages; by contrast, whites sought wages that were only 10 percent higher. However, Petterson argues that these results do not necessarily reveal "cultural differences in willingness to work" among blacks because the greater discrepancy in reservation wages and previous wages may simply be a function of their greater concentration in previous low-wage jobs.[68] Indeed, Petterson finds no evidence that the reservation wages of blacks are excessively high. "In fact the opposite may be true," he states. Blacks in the ninth decile of the wage distribution—that is, those who are paid less than 90 percent of what the general workforce earns—report a mean reservation wage of only $5.41, lower than the mean of $6.19 for comparable whites. "The race difference is even greater in the last decile," states Petterson. "Evidently the higher reservation wages relative to past wages reported by blacks are due to their concentration at the lower end of the past-wage distribution. At most levels of previous wages, I find no significant differences in reservation wages."[69]

Moreover, Petterson found no support for the cultural argument that low-skilled black job seekers "experience longer jobless spells because of their excessive reservation wages."[70] Indeed, his results reveal that reported reservation wages do not have a significant impact on the duration of joblessness. Although low-skilled blacks have a clear set of norms defining fair and unfair wages, these norms tend not to be binding when they are confronted with realistic job situations. What they say they will do is frequently not consistent with what they actually do when receiving a job offer. In a related study, Petterson found that just one or two weeks after stating their reservation wages, 30.8 percent of white workers and 41.5 percent of black workers accepted jobs with wages below their reported reservation wages.[71]

Although Petterson's research shows that there are good alternatives to the subculture-of-resistance arguments, one cannot conclude from his findings that black and white youths do not draw a line on certain low-wage jobs. They may decline the option of working alongside recent immigrants for subminimum wages in filthy sweatshop jobs, consistent with Orlando Patterson's arguments that young black males will refuse jobs that at least some immigrants are willing to take. Nonetheless, as Petterson argues, "despite the dramatic decline in the wages earned by disadvantaged workers, many hope to earn modest but decent wages comparable to those still earned by at least some of the more fortunate low-skilled workers. With few options, however, they often settle for less."[72] This astute point is overlooked in Mead's unsupported assertion that young black workers are unwilling to accept menial employment.[73]

If the evidence to support arguments concerning a subculture of defeatism and a subculture of resistance is at best mixed, Sandra Smith provides a compelling and nuanced cultural analysis of other factors that contribute to the complex and often difficult world of work inhabited by low-skilled blacks. Smith conducted in-depth interviews with 105 black men and women in Michigan between the ages of twenty and forty who had no more than a high school education so that she could examine the informal personal networks of low-skilled black job holders and job seekers.[74]

Before we consider her findings, it might be useful to point out that Smith's study was motivated in part to test some of the intriguing findings revealed by our earlier Chicago research. As I pointed out in Chapter 1, the breakdown of informal job information networks aggravates the problems of job spatial mismatch.[75] This means that people who live in areas of concentrated poverty are both physically and socially isolated from jobs. In our Chicago research we found that overall, the personal friendship networks of blacks (both male and female) are very limited. For example, the poor blacks we talked to in our fieldwork were less likely to have at least one employed close friend than were Mexican immigrants of similar income and education. Because these people lacked friends with jobs, they tended not to hear about possible job opportunities or even different types of employment. This form of social isolation handicapped the residents of inner-city black neighborhoods; as many stable working neighbors drifted away, the ties connecting the remaining residents to the world of work came undone. Analysis of our ethnographic data for the remaining poor and often unemployed residents revealed that "social contacts were a useful means of gaining informal work to help make ends meet but far less often successful in helping with steady employment in the formal economy; networks existed but largely lacked the capacity to help lift residents into the formal labor market."[76]

Moreover, our data on job search behavior revealed that black men and women in the inner city were less likely than Mexican immigrants to report that they had received help from a friend or relative in obtaining their current job. The job search strategies that inner-city black residents most frequently reported using were filling out an application at a place of business and seeking assistance at an employment office. Seldom did anyone report that they had heard about a job from an acquaintance or a friend.

Smith's data provide new information to help explain why informal job networks among blacks were less useful in helping job seekers find employment in the formal economy. She found that distrust on the part of black job holders and the defensive individualism typical of black job seekers profoundly affected the use of job referrals in the search for employment. She points out that the neighborhoods of the black poor are "characterized by chronic poverty and a history of exploitation" and tend to feed the inclination to distrust, "inhibiting the development of mutually beneficial cooperative relationships such as those that facilitate the job-matching process."[77] The cooperation between job seekers and job holders is thwarted by a lack of mutual trust. Thus, low-skilled black job seekers are frequently unable to use their friendships, acquaintances, and family ties—their informal network—to gain employment. Black job holders were reluctant to refer their relatives and friends for jobs because they feared that their own reputations with employers could be jeopardized if the work of the people they recommended was substandard.

Accordingly, instead of exhibiting a subculture of defeatism or resistance, Smith found that her low-skilled subjects displayed a discourse of individualism. On the one hand, job holders justified denying assistance to their relatives and friends by saying that these individuals lacked motivation and individual responsibility. On the other hand, many low-skilled job seekers, particularly black males—"cognizant of how they are perceived by others in their social milieu" and concerned about being demeaned for their unemployment—hesitated to approach their peers for referrals.[78] This "go it alone" approach proves enormously self-defeating because employers in low-skilled labor markets rely heavily on personal referrals. Smith's analysis provides an excellent example of how cultural frames (shared visions of human behavior developed from the micro-level processes of meaning making and decision making) orient action—in this case, the limited use of job referrals.

If there was a lack of cooperation between black job seekers and job holders, Smith also found contention and distrust between young, black male job seekers and the staff members of a state job center. The common assumption among the staff members was that the young black men did not really want to make the effort required to find jobs. This assumption hurt the employment prospects of the job seekers because the job center, a private contractor hired by the state of Michigan, was concerned about meeting performance quotas and therefore tended to screen out the riskiest candidates—those who had the greatest employment obstacles and required the most help.[79] Smith's study further substantiates the importance of combining a definitive cultural analysis (exploring the effects of a tendency to distrust and the discourse of individualism in the black community) with a structural explanation (focusing on the impact of discriminatory actions of the staff members of a job center) to account for the employment outcomes of low-skilled, young black males.

Conclusion

In the previous chapter I argued, on the basis of available evidence, that structural explanations of concentrated poverty in the inner city have far greater significance than cultural arguments, even though neither should be considered in isolation if we are seeking a comprehensive understanding of racial inequality because structural and cultural forces often interact in affecting the experiences and chances in life of particular racial group members. The evidence discussed in this chapter supports a similar conclusion: structural explanations of the economic woes of low-skilled black men are far more significant than cultural arguments, even though structural and cultural forces jointly restrict black male progress in some situations.

The disproportionate number of low-skilled black males in this country is one of the legacies of historical segregation and discrimination. However, aside from the effects of current segregation and discrimination, including those caused by employer bias, I highlighted a number of impersonal economic forces that have contributed to the incredibly high jobless rate of low-skilled black males and their correspondingly low incomes. These forces include the decreased relative demand for low-skilled labor caused by the computer revolution, the globalization of economic activity, the declining manufacturing sector, and the growth of service industries in which most of the new jobs for workers with limited skills and education are concentrated.

I noted that the shift to service industries has created a new set of problems for low-skilled black males because those industries feature jobs that require workers to serve and relate to consumers. Why are such requirements a problem for black men? Simply because employers believe that women and recent immigrants of both genders are better suited than black males, especially those with prison records, for such jobs. This image has been created partly by cultural shifts in national attitudes that reflected concerns about the growth of violence in the ghettos through the 1960s and '70s. In the eyes of many Americans, black males symbolized this violence. Cries for "law and order" resulted in a more punitive criminal justice system and a dramatic increase in black male incarceration.

Cultural arguments have been advanced to explain the social and economic woes of low-skilled black males, but the evidence is mixed. For example, a number of studies have associated black joblessness with high reservation wages, the lowest wages that a worker is willing to accept. Nonetheless, one of the more compelling studies found no significant relationship between the reservation wages of black men and the duration of joblessness. The findings in an important recent study, however, clearly suggest that chronic poverty and exploitation in poor black neighborhoods tend to feed inclinations to distrust. These cultural traits undermine the development of cooperative relationships that are so vital in informal job networks. Black workers in the inner city tend to be less willing to recommend friends and relatives for jobs that become available. Thus, the structural problem of employer job discrimination and the cultural inclination to distrust combine to severely handicap low-skilled, black male workers, especially those with prison records.

CHAPTER 4

THE FRAGMENTATION OF THE POOR BLACK FAMILY

In 1965, a report entitled "The Negro Family: The Case for National Action" was published by the assistant secretary of labor, Daniel Patrick Moynihan, who in 1976 would be elected the Democratic senator from New York. In what quickly became known as "the Moynihan report," the author asserted that racial inequality, combined with the breakdown of the black family, was creating a "new crisis in race relations." Moynihan combined structural and cultural arguments to analyze the deteriorating state of black families. The report created a firestorm of controversy due in part to the racial climate and popular ideology at the time it was published. America had moved against segregation in public schools in the 1954 case *Brown v. Board of Education*, and other segregationist practices had been successfully attacked in the courts and influenced by legislation through the first half of the 1960s. The legal battle against discriminatory practices was welcomed by many but was still hardly universally embraced. Many Americans were skeptical about how much could and should change between blacks and whites in America, even while citizens with more liberal attitudes about race relations supported the end of segregation.

Given the volatility of race relations, liberal critics believed that Moynihan's cultural arguments amounted to blaming African Americans for their own misfortune. This criticism ignored Moynihan's careful attention to structural causes of inequality, and it created a backlash against the report that essentially shut down meaningful conversation about the role of culture in shaping racial outcomes. The Moynihan report is a particularly pertinent subject for a discussion of the black family because it not only anticipated later developments in black family fragmentation, but the controversy it generated clearly made the African American family the central focus of the structure-versus-culture debate.

In a *New York Times* obituary for Daniel Patrick Moynihan in March 2003, I was quoted as saying that the Moynihan report is an important and prophetic document.[1] I still stand by that statement. The report is important because it continues to be a reference for studies on the black family. It is prophetic because Moynihan's predictions about the fragmentation of the African American family and its connection to inner-city poverty were largely borne out.

Because the Moynihan report was an internal document written for officials in the executive branch of government, not the general public, its findings and commentary were not edited to minimize the chances of press distortions and the odds of offending civil rights groups. Dramatic statements made in the report drew press attention and were often taken out of context. For example, in his chapter entitled "The Tangle of Pathology," Moynihan boldly stated, "At the heart of the deterioration of the fabric of Negro society is the deterioration of the Negro family. It is the fundamental weakness of the Negro community at the present time"; and "at the center of the tangle of pathology is the weakness of the family structure. Once or twice removed, it will be found to be the principal source of most of the aberrant, inadequate, or antisocial behavior that did not establish, but now serves to perpetuate the cycle of poverty and deprivation."[2]

Reporters and columnists organized their coverage around the attention-grabbing statements on the breakdown of the black family, and readers who had not read the actual document often had no idea that Moynihan had devoted an entire chapter to the root causes of family fragmentation, including urbanization, unemployment, poverty, and Jim Crow segregation. A *Washington Post* bylined article noted, according to "White House sources," that the Watts riot in 1964—a race riot in a suburb of Los Angeles—strengthened President Johnson's "feeling of the urgent need to restore Negro families' stability."[3] Accordingly, as Lee Rainwater and William L. Yancey observed, by the time many critics, including black critics, got around to reading the report, they "could no longer see it with fresh eyes but were instead heavily influenced by their exposure to the press coverage, particularly as this coverage tied the report to an official 'explanation' for Watts."[4]

The critical reaction of many African Americans to the report was also influenced by racial sentiments in the black community flowing from the emergence of the Black Power movement in the mid-1960s. Some blacks were highly critical of the report's emphasis on social pathologies within poor black neighborhoods not simply because such a conclusion carried with it potential for deep embarrassment. They believed that such a view of black life conflicted with their claim that blacks were developing a community power base that could become a major force in

American society and would reflect the strength and vitality of the black community.

This critical reaction to the analysis of a prominent white social scientist and politician reflected a new definition, description, and explanation of the black condition that accompanied the emergence of the Black Power movement. This new approach, proclaimed as the "black perspective," signaled an ideological shift from interracialism to black solidarity. It first gained currency among militant black spokespersons in the mid-1960s; by the early 1970s it had become a recurrent theme in the writings of a number of black academics and intellectuals.[5] Although the black perspective represented a variety of views and arguments on issues of race, the trumpeting of racial pride and self-affirmation was common to many of the writings and speeches on the subject.[6]

In this atmosphere of racial chauvinism, a series of scholarly studies proclaiming a black perspective were published. The arguments set forth made clear a substantial and fundamental shift in both the tone and focus of race relations scholarship. Consistent with the emphasis on black glorification and the quest for self-affirmation, analyses that described some aspects of ghetto life as pathological tended to be rejected in favor of those that emphasized black strengths. Arguments that focused on the deterioration of the poor black family were dismissed in favor of those that extolled the strengths of black families. Thus, black-perspective proponents reinterpreted behavior that Daniel Moynihan, psychologist Kenneth Clark, and sociologist Lee Rainwater had described as self-destructive and instead proclaimed it as creative in the sense that many blacks were displaying the ability to survive and even flourish in a ghetto milieu. Poor African American families were described as resilient and were seen as imaginatively adapting to an oppressive society.

The logic put forth by proponents of the black-perspective explanation is interesting because it does not even acknowledge self-destructive behavior in the ghetto. This is a unique response to the dominant American belief system's emphasis on individual deficiencies, rather than the structure of opportunity, as causes of poverty and welfare. Instead of challenging the validity of the underlying assumptions of this belief system, this approach sidesteps the issue altogether by denying that social dislocations in the inner city represent any special problem. Researchers who emphasized these dislocations—such as persistent unemployment, crime, and drug use—were denounced, even when their work rejected the assumption of individual responsibility for poverty and welfare and focused instead on the structural roots of these problems.[7]

The vitriolic attacks and acrimonious debate that characterized this controversy proved to be too intimidating to scholars, particularly to liberal scholars. Accordingly, in the early 1970s, unlike the mid-1960s, there was little motivation to develop a research agenda that pursued the structural and cultural causes of social and economic problems in the inner-city ghetto. Indeed, in the aftermath of this controversy and in an effort to protect their work from the charge of racism or of "blaming the victim," many liberal social scientists tended to avoid describing any behavior that could be construed as unflattering or stigmatizing to people of color. As a result, in the years following the initial controversy of the Moynihan report until the mid-1980s, social problems in the inner-city ghetto did not attract serious research attention from US social scientists.

Although research on urban poverty has mushroomed in the last several years, lingering effects of the Moynihan controversy on the willingness of social scientists to pursue a cultural analysis of life in poverty still remain. We will discuss this issue shortly, but first I must briefly put Moynihan's concerns in current perspective, to highlight the ways in which the report was prophetic.

Several trends that had earlier worried Moynihan have become much more pronounced. One-quarter of all nonwhite births were to unmarried women in 1965, the year Moynihan wrote the report on the Negro family, and by 1996 the proportion of black children born outside of marriage had reached a high of 70 percent; it then dipped slightly to 69 percent in 2005 (see Figure 4.1).[8] And in 1965 a single woman headed 25 percent of all nonwhite families; by 1996, however, the proportion of all black families headed by a single woman had swelled to 47 percent, dropping slightly to 45 percent in 2006 (see Figure 4.2).[9]

Figure 4.1

Nonmarital Births among Blacks*

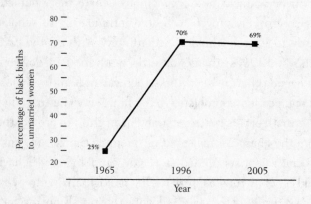

*Statistics were not available for blacks in 1965. It is estimated that blacks comprised roughly 90 percent of those classified as "nonwhite."

US Department of Health, Education, and Welfare, *Trends in Illegitimacy: 1940–1965*, National Vital Statistics System, Series 21, No. 15 (Washington, DC: Government Printing Office, 1974); US Department of Health and Human Services, *Nonmarital Childbearing in the United States, 1940–1999*, National Vital Statistics Reports, Vol. 48, No. 16 (Washington, DC: Government Printing Office, 2000); and US Department of Health and Human Services, *Births: Preliminary Data for 2005* (Washington, DC: Government Printing Office, 2006).

Figure 4.2

Black* Families Headed by a Single Mother

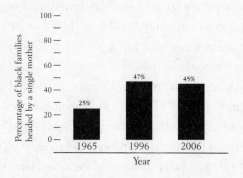

*Statistics were not available for blacks in 1965. It is estimated that blacks comprised roughly 90 percent of those classified as "nonwhite."

US Bureau of the Census, *Current Population Survey* (Washington, DC: Government Printing Office, 1996); and US Bureau of the Census, *Current Population Survey* (Washington, DC: Government Printing Office, 2006).

One reason for Moynihan's concern about the decline in the rate of marriage among blacks is that children living in single-parent families in the United States, especially families in which the parents have never been married to each other, suffer from many more disadvantages than those who are raised in married-parent families. A study relying on longitudinal data (data collected on a specific group over a substantial period of time) found that, in the United States, persistently poor families (defined as having family incomes below the poverty line during at least eight years in a ten-year period) tended to be headed by women, and 31 percent of all persistently poor households were headed by nonelderly *black* women.[10] This is an astounding figure, considering that African Americans account for just 12.4 percent of the entire US population.[11]

As sociologist Kathryn Edin pointed out, "more children are poor today than at any time since before Lyndon Johnson's War on Poverty began three decades ago. Children living in households headed by single mothers are America's poorest demographic group. This fact is not surprising, since low-skilled single mothers who work seldom earn enough to bring their families out of poverty and most cannot get child support, medical benefits, housing subsidies, or cheap child care."[12]

In 2006, whereas the median income of married-couple families with children was $72,948, the median income of single-parent families in which the mother was divorced was $35,217. For families in which the mother had never been married, the median income was only $18,111. Likewise, whereas less than one-tenth of children in husband–wife families were living below the poverty line, nearly one-quarter of those living with divorced mothers and over half of those living with mothers who had never been married were classified as poor.[13] Recent research firmly supports the idea that some of the increase in the child poverty rate can be attributed to changes in family structure (i.e., the gradual shift from married-couple to single-parent families).[14] Finally, longitudinal studies also revealed that before passage of the welfare reform legislation in 1996, mothers who had never been married received assistance from Aid to Families with Dependent Children (AFDC) for a significantly longer period than did separated or divorced mothers.[15]

In addition to the strong connection linking single parenthood with poverty and welfare receipt, the available research indicates that children from low-income households without fathers present are more likely to be school dropouts, become teenage parents, receive lower earnings in young adulthood, be welfare recipients, and experience cognitive, emotional, and social problems. Moreover, daughters who grow up in single-parent households are more likely to establish single-parent households themselves than are those raised in married-couple households. And finally, single-parent households tend to exert less control over the behavior of their adolescent children.[16]

Although statistics that record nonmarital births provide some sense of the extent to which mothers are having children outside of marriage, they do not provide an accurate picture of how many mothers are actually parenting alone. The reason is that nonmarital-birth statistics measure marital status at the time of birth only, and do not take into account other types of co-parenting relationships, such as couples who marry after the birth of a child. For example, among women with nonmarital first births, 82 percent of whites, 62 percent of Hispanics, and 59 percent of blacks married by age forty.[17] However, according to one recent study of fragile families in seven cities, when the focus was low-income minority families, three-fourths of which were black, only 15 percent of unmarried mothers were married by the time of their child's first birthday.[18]

The decrease in the proportion of married parents in the previous forty years had been partially offset by an increase in the proportion of parents who were unmarried but maintained a relationship, as either cohabiting or visiting partners. However, despite the extent to which cohabiting- and visiting-partner relationships offset the decline in married-couple families, black mothers in the inner city are far more likely than mothers of other ethnic groups to reside in households in which no other adults are present, and these mothers face greater challenges in raising children. Whereas 44 percent of the black women living with their children in Chicago's inner city had no other adults in the household when our research was conducted in the late 1980s, only 6.5 percent of comparable Mexican American women were the sole adults in their households. Furthermore, inner-city black women whose children were under twelve years of age were eight times more likely than comparable Mexican American women to live in a single-adult household.

Analyzing data from our study, Martha Van Haitsma found that "network differences translate into childcare differences. Mexican women with young children are significantly more likely than their black counterparts to have regular childcare provided by a friend or relative."[19] The high proportion of two-adult Mexican American households with working fathers, particularly among immigrant Mexicans, may be an important factor in the mother's greater access to networks of child care.

Also in our study, the high percentage of black mothers who lived with young children in a single-adult household was associated with problems finding and keeping a job—what social scientists call labor force attachment.[20] If a single mother in Chicago's inner city lived in a *co-residential household*—that is, a household that included at least one other adult—and received informal child care, she significantly improved her chances of entering the labor force. Inner-city mothers who were not on welfare, lived in a co-residential household, and received informal child care had a very high (90 percent) probability of labor force activity; those who maintained sole-adult households and did not receive informal child care had a much lower (60 percent) probability of working. Of the 12 percent of inner-city welfare mothers who candidly reported that they worked at least part-time—probably in the informal economy—those who lived in a co-residential household and received informal child care were more than five times as likely to work as were those who lived in single households and did not receive informal child care.[21]

Given the sharp increase in single-parent families and out-of-wedlock births in the African American community and the research showing a relationship between these trends and economic hardships, few serious scholars would maintain that Moynihan's concerns about the changes in the black family were unjustified, even though the percentage of nonmarital births and single-mother families has increased among whites and Latinos as well.[22] What continues to be disputed is how we account for the fragmentation of the African American family. What is often overlooked is that Moynihan attempted to synthesize structural and cultural analyses to understand the dynamics of poor black families. This relationship between structure and culture is explored in the remainder of this chapter.

The Role of Structural Factors

The explanations most often heard in the public debate over the last several decades associate the increase in out-of-wedlock births and single-parent families with welfare. The general public discussions and proposals for welfare reform reflected a wide assumption that there was a direct causal link between the level or generosity of welfare benefits and the likelihood that a young woman would bear a child outside of marriage. The fact that welfare recipients received benefits for their children was assumed to provide an incentive for additional childbearing. This widespread belief led several states, as part of the 1996 welfare reform, to adopt a family cap policy that stopped increasing benefits for additional babies born. In addition, welfare policy is thought to discourage marriage because of the way income limits are used to qualify someone for benefits. In 1998 the federal poverty line was $13,133 for a single parent with two children, and it was just $3,400 more for a dual-parent household with two children ($16,530). Therefore, it is very easy for a dual-parent family to disqualify itself from welfare, even if earnings are very low.[23] Accordingly, welfare has been construed as a disincentive for marriage.

However, scientific evidence gathered in the early 1990s offered little support for these claims.[24] Research examining the association between the generosity of welfare benefits and out-of-wedlock childbearing and teen pregnancy prior to the enactment of welfare reform in 1996 indicated that benefit levels had no significant effect on the likelihood that African American girls and women would have children outside of marriage; likewise, benefit levels had either no significant effect or only a small effect on the odds that whites would have children outside of marriage. There is no evidence to suggest that welfare was a major factor in the rise of childbearing outside of marriage.

The corollary to the "welfare encourages childbirth outside of marriage" assumption is that decreases in welfare benefits also hinder nonmarital births. But this does not hold true. The states with the largest declines in AFDC benefits did not register the greatest slowdown in out-of-wedlock births.[25] The rate of out-of-wedlock teen childbearing had nearly doubled between 1975 and 1996, the year welfare reform was enacted, even though the real value of AFDC, food stamps, and Medicaid during that period had fallen, after adjustment for inflation. Indeed, while the real value of cash welfare benefits had plummeted from the mid-1970s to the mid-1990s, not only had out-of-wedlock childbearing increased, but the tendency for partners to marry following the birth of their child had decreased as well.[26]

In *The Truly Disadvantaged*, I argued that the sharp increase in black male joblessness since 1970 accounts in large measure for the rise in the rate of single-parent families, and that because jobless rates are highest in the inner-city ghetto, rates of single parenthood are also highest there. Thus, many of the structural factors that have contributed to the increase in joblessness among low-skilled black males and the corresponding sharp decline in their income discussed in the previous chapters—the decreased relative demand for low-skilled labor caused by the computer revolution, the growing internationalization of low-skilled labor, the decline of the manufacturing sector, and the growth of service industries—logically extend to a discussion of the factors that contribute to the fragmentation of black families.

Whereas almost 27.5 percent of young African American men nationwide (ages eighteen to twenty-nine) with annual earnings of over $35,000 were married in 2006, the marriage ratio decreased steadily for those earning less than that—21.7 percent for those earning between $25,000 and $35,000, 15.3 percent for those earning between $15,000 and $25,000, 7.6 percent for those earning between $2,000 and $10,000, and only 7.5 percent for those with no reported earnings.[27]

However, research on the relationship between male employment and rates of marriage and single parenthood has yielded mixed findings. Although there is a strong association between rates of marriage and both employment status and earnings at any given point in time, national longitudinal studies suggest that these factors account for a relatively small proportion of the overall *decline* in marriage among African Americans. Harvard professor Christopher Jencks points out that the decline in the proportion of African American men who were married and living with their wives was almost as large among those who had worked throughout the previous years as among black men in general.[28] In addition, studies have shown only modest support for the hypothesis linking the sharp rise in poor, single-parent families to the declining employment status and income of young black men.[29]

However, these studies are based on national data, not data specific to inner-city neighborhoods where many experiences relate to race and poverty. How much of the decline in the black marriage rate in the inner city can be accounted for by the increasing joblessness among black males? Our study of family life and poverty in Chicago's inner city was not a longitudinal study, but we did collect retrospective (or life history) marriage and employment data that help us estimate trends over time. An analysis of respondents' retrospective data comparing the employment experiences of different age groups (cohorts) revealed that marriage rates had dropped much more sharply among jobless black fathers than among employed black fathers. But this drop applies only to the younger cohorts. Analyzing data from our survey, Mark Testa and Marilyn Krogh found that although employment had no significant effect on the likelihood that black single fathers ages thirty-two to forty-four would eventually marry, it increased that likelihood by eight times for single fathers eighteen to thirty-one years old.[30]

Joblessness among black men is a significant factor in their delayed entry into marriage and in the decreasing rates of marriage after a child has been born, and this relationship has been exacerbated by sharp increases in incarceration that in turn lead to continued joblessness. Nevertheless, much of the decline in marriages in the inner city, including marriages that occur after a child has been born, remains unexplained when only structural factors are examined.

The Role of Cultural Factors

Even though whites and Latinos have also experienced an increase in the percentage of nonmarital births and single-mother families, although at a slower rate than among African Americans, social scientists continue to argue about whether unique cultural factors may account for the fragmentation of the African American family. As mentioned earlier, the controversy over the Moynihan report resulted in a persistent taboo on cultural explanations to help explain social problems in the poor black community.

If the public release of the Moynihan report was untimely in terms of the changing racial climate, it was also unfortunately published during heated debate over anthropologist Oscar Lewis's work on the culture of poverty. Although Lewis's work had been conducted among Spanish-speaking persons in Mexico, Puerto Rico, and New York City, his argument that poverty is passed from generation to generation through learned behaviors and attitudes was irresistibly attractive—or repellent—to persons interested in the plight of poor black Americans. Indeed, the Moynihan report quickly became a reference point for debates about the culture of poverty. The link between the report and Lewis's theory was made especially explicit following the publication of an article and later a book, both titled "Blaming the Victim," written by the Boston psychologist and civil rights activist William Ryan as a critique of the Moynihan report.[31] "Blaming the victim" became a slogan repeatedly used by critics of the culture-of-poverty thesis, and they made repeated reference to the Moynihan report when voicing their criticisms.

Relying on participant observation and life history data to analyze Latin American poverty, Oscar Lewis described the culture of poverty as "both an adaptation and a reaction of the poor to their marginal position in a class-stratified, highly individuated capitalistic society." However, he also noted that once the culture of poverty comes into existence, "it tends to perpetuate itself from generation to generation because of its effect on the children. By the time slum children are age six or seven they have usually absorbed the basic values and attitudes of their subculture and are not psychologically geared to take full advantage of changing conditions or increased opportunities which may occur in their lifetime."[32] Although Lewis later modified his position by placing more weight on external societal forces than on self-perpetuating cultural traits to explain the behavior of the poor, conservative social scientists embellished the idea that poverty is a product of "deeply ingrained habits" that are unlikely to change following improvements in external conditions.[33]

Although Moynihan devoted an entire chapter of the report to structural causes for the fragmentation of the black family and the downward spiral of low-skilled black males, a close reading of his report does reveal an implicit culture-of-poverty explanation as well. Like Oscar Lewis, Moynihan relates cultural patterns to structural factors and then discusses how these patterns come to influence other aspects of behavior. In the concluding chapter of his report, for example, Moynihan states that the situation of the black family "may indeed have begun to feed on itself." To illustrate, he notes that from 1948 to 1962, the unemployment rate among black males and the number of new AFDC cases were very highly correlated. After 1962, however, the trend reversed itself for the first time. The number of new AFDC cases continued to rise, but black male unemployment declined.[34] "With this one statistical correlation, by far the most highly publicized in the Report," states the historian Alice O'Connor, "Moynihan sealed the argument that the 'pathology' had become self-perpetuating: pathology, here measured as welfare 'dependency,' was no longer correlated with the unemployment rate; it was going up on its own."[35] Also like Oscar Lewis, Moynihan talks about the adverse effects of children being exposed to the cultural environment or, as he puts it, to the tangle of pathology in the ghetto.

Unlike many conservative social scientists, however, Moynihan does not imply that the fragmentation of black families and the associated problems are immutable and cannot be changed through social policy. In addition, his implicit cultural argument on the impact of black family fragmentation, which many would associate with the culture of poverty, is, to repeat, part of a complex thesis on the black family that combines structural and cultural factors.

According to Orlando Patterson, the resistance to a cultural analysis of the fragmentation of the black family has been caused in no small measure by reactions to the Moynihan report.[36] This reaction resulted in a lack of attention to possible cultural continuities in the black family that may be traceable back to slavery. It also led to a lack of understanding of the role of culture in accounting for how black people respond to poverty, and indeed how cultural practices may contribute to either the increase or reduction of poverty.

Let's briefly discuss the issue of cultural continuities. As Patterson correctly points out, scholars such as W. E. B. Du Bois, E. Franklin Frazier, and Kenneth B. Clark exemplify a long tradition of African American scholarship that partly explains the distinctive African American gender and familial patterns that follow from the experiences of slavery. Following the Moynihan report, however, "the ideological and scholarly tide turned sharply away from this claim of continuity toward a denial of any such connection."[37]

The most persuasive and widely cited critique of this view was a book by the historian Herbert G. Gutman, who challenged Moynihan's view that the African American family was weak, disorganized, and matrifocal (meaning that women occupied a central position) as it emerged from slavery.[38] Relying on census data and historical documents, including letters and diaries, Gutman argued that far from being weak, black American families had been strong and resilient after emancipation. In the early twentieth century, most were married-couple families and a majority of the children were born within marriage. "In the 50 years after emancipation," Gutman wrote, "most African-American families were headed by a husband and wife, most eventually married, and most children lived with both parents."[39]

However, social scientists from the University of Pennsylvania seriously challenged Gutman's thesis in two major studies: one by Samuel H. Preston and his colleagues, the other by S. Philip Morgan and several of his colleagues.[40] Each study is based on public use samples from the US Census Bureau, which were released after the publication of Gutman's book. These new data sets allow for a finer-grained analysis of the "consistency of various census items and of the link among marital status, marital histories, current fertility and fertility history."[41]

Using data from the public use samples, Preston and his colleagues revealed that the straightforward census tabulations that Gutman had relied on had serious flaws. They show that widowhood was overreported for both younger and older black women, and that some of the overreporting reflected attempts to account for births outside of marriage. "Furthermore, when compared to reconstruction based on women's ages at marriage and on husbands' mortality," state the authors, "census reports contained far too many first marriages of short duration. This latter evidence suggests that previous unions were often omitted and that marital turnover was faster than implied even by the high percentages of women reported as married."[42] Preston and his colleagues therefore conclude that Gutman's portrait of stable African American families in the rural South prior to their mass migration to the urban North is overstated.

Following this study, Morgan and his colleagues found distinct differences in living arrangements between native-born white and black Americans at the start of the twentieth century that "were geographically pervasive—they are unmistakable in the North and South and in both rural and urban areas."[43] Socioeconomic factors such as poverty, women's employment, and the lower earnings of African American males accounted for some of these racial differences. But it is clear from this study that these factors, although clearly necessary in any explanatory framework, were hardly sufficient to explain the differences. Indeed, both studies argued that more attention should be given to cultural/historical factors. For example, Morgan and colleagues point out that despite studies showing cultural/historical continuity in the linguistic and religious behaviors of African Americans and despite studies of Caribbean societies that take historical and cultural influences on family patterns seriously, "most historians of the African-American family have gone to great lengths to discount the possibility of cultural continuity between African and African-American family systems."[44]

Morgan and his colleagues note that some contemporary historians argue that antebellum slavery reinforced the sub-Saharan African pattern of strong ties and obligations to extended kin. "Despite the absence of any legal standing for slave 'marriage,' slaves were able to maintain strong familial bonds, especially kin bonds. These traditions could make spouse absence and separation more acceptable among African Americans than among whites,"[45] and that persistent residential segregation and the lack of racial interaction in the social, economic, and cultural spheres could maintain or reinforce such differences. From a comparative perspective, however, it is difficult to follow this reasoning. For example, as we shall soon see, Mexican Americans also value extended family and yet do not have a high tolerance for paternal absence.[46] Morgan and his colleagues do not address such issues, but they do conclude that an adequate explanation of contemporary African American family patterns requires carefully "synthesized arguments that weave together the influence of demographic, socioeconomic, and cultural/historical factors."[47]

Orlando Patterson later made the same point in his provocative book *Rituals of Blood*.[48] In his zeal to demonstrate the importance of cultural continuity, however, Patterson downplays the importance of social/economic factors such as male joblessness in accounting for family fragmentation among African Americans, leaving unexplored the puzzle pointed out by David Ellwood and Christopher Jencks: "why these cultural legacies should suddenly have become more important in the last half of the twentieth century."[49] Patterson argues that the economic problems experienced by inner-city residents do not sufficiently explain current trends in the formation of the black family.

Following Patterson's logic, if historical research suggests cultural/historical continuity in the linguistic and religious behaviors of African Americans, we should not dismiss cultural continuity in trying to fully explain family patterns in the African American community. However, cultural continuities are difficult to substantiate. What mechanisms transmit weak family structure across generations? With linguistic and religious traditions it is pretty clear how intergenerational continuity is maintained, especially when families are segregated by race and class and have limited contacts with other groups. However, how does one separate factors influenced by cultural continuities from factors derived from situational and contextual factors such as joblessness and persistent poverty?

Concerns about cultural continuity are even raised by scholars who urge that more attention be given to the role of culture in the study of human behavior. Their major concern is that the proponents of cultural/historical continuity tend to define culture as a specific set of orientations and practices characteristic of a particular group. In their perceptive paper on how culture matters for the understanding of poverty, Michèle Lamont and Mario Small, two prominent cultural sociologists, question the idea that racial or ethnic groups "have" a culture "in the sense of sets of values or attitudes that all or most members of a racial or ethnic (or class) group share."[50]

Pointing out that the differences within a group are often larger than the differences between distinct groups (e.g., differences between the black middle class and the black lower class on a range of cultural attributes may be greater than differences between blacks and whites per se), Lamont and Small maintain that it is not helpful to speak of an African American culture that differs from an Asian culture or a Euro-American culture in the study of racial differences in poverty. "Instead of imputing a shared culture to groups," they argue, it is better to examine empirically "the range of frames through which people make sense of their reality and how they use them to orient their action."[51] Lamont and Small further argue that cultural "frames do not cause behavior so much as make it possible or likely."[52] In other words, cultural frames are necessary but not sufficient explanations for behavior. For the purpose of pursuing a cultural analysis of life in poverty, I fully agree.

The cultural continuity thesis may have merit, but there is not enough evidence to corroborate or confirm it at this time. In other words, the relative importance of the combination of cultural continuity and contemporary socioeconomic factors in accounting for black family patterns remains an open question that can be best answered through careful empirical research.

The decline in the rate of marriage among inner-city black parents in the last several decades is a function not simply of deepening scarcity of jobs for low-skilled workers or of changing attitudes toward sex and marriage in society at large, but of, as Testa emphasizes, "the interaction between material and cultural constraints."[53] The important point is that "variation in the moral evaluations that different sociocultural groups attach to premarital sex, out-of-wedlock pregnancy, and nonmarital parenthood affects the importance of economic considerations in a person's decision to marry."[54] That is, discouraging economic conditions tend to reinforce any tolerance for having children without marriage or even partnering. The weaker the norms are against premarital sex, out-of-wedlock pregnancy, and nonmarital parenthood, the more economic considerations affect decisions to marry.

The data we collected in the late 1980s in our random survey of nearly 2,500 poor and nonpoor African American, Latino, and white residents in Chicago's inner-city neighborhoods shed light on this relationship.[55] Only 28 percent of the African American parents aged eighteen to forty-four were married when they were interviewed in 1987 and 1988, compared with 75 percent of the Mexican American parents, 61 percent of the white parents, and 45 percent of the Puerto Rican parents. African Americans in these neighborhoods suffered from higher levels of joblessness and higher rates of concentrated poverty (the percentage of poor families in a neighborhood), which accounted for some of the differences. But even when ethnic-group variations in work activity, poverty concentration, education, and family structure were taken into account, significant differences between inner-city blacks and the other groups, especially the Mexican Americans, remained.[56] Accordingly, it is reasonable to consider the influence of cultural variables in accounting for some of these differences.

A brief comparison between inner-city blacks and inner-city Mexican Americans (many of whom are immigrants) in terms of family perspectives provides some evidence of cultural differences. Marriage and family ties are subjects of "frequent and intense discourse" among Mexican American immigrants.[57] Mexicans come to the United States with a clear conception of a traditional family unit that features men as breadwinners. Although extramarital affairs by men are tolerated, "a pregnant, unmarried woman is a source of opprobrium, anguish, or great concern."[58] Pressure is applied by the kin of both parents for the couple to enter into marriage. Religion undoubtedly plays a role in Mexican American marital sanctions. Mexicans have been strongly influenced by Roman Catholicism, a religion that discourages divorce and out-of-wedlock pregnancies. It is therefore reasonable to assume that the Mexican cultural framing of marriage is significantly influenced by religious beliefs and other traditional conceptions of what constitutes an appropriate family unit.

The intensity of the commitment to the marital bond among Mexican immigrants will very likely decline, the longer they remain in the United States and are exposed to US norms and the changing opportunity structures for men and women. Indeed, Mexican American women born in the United States are significantly more likely to experience a marital disruption (i.e., divorce or separation) compared to Mexican American women born in Mexico (40.9 percent compared to 13.1 percent, respectively).[59]

Nonetheless, cultural arrangements reflect structural realities. In comparison with inner-city blacks, inner-city Mexican immigrants have a stronger attachment to the labor force—they have come, after all, a very long way to find work—as well as stronger households, networks, and neighborhoods. Therefore, as long as these differences exist, attitudes toward the family and family formation among inner-city blacks and Mexican immigrants will contrast noticeably.

Ethnographic data from our Chicago study revealed that the relationships between inner-city black men and women, whether in a marital or nonmarital situation, were often fractious and antagonistic. Inner-city black women routinely said they distrusted men

and felt strongly that black men lacked dedication to their partners and children.[60] They argued that black males are hopeless as
either husbands or fathers and that more of their time is spent on
the streets than at home. As one woman, an unmarried mother
of three children from a high-poverty neighborhood on the South
Side, put it, "and most of the men don't have jobs . . . but if things
were equal it really wouldn't matter, would it? I mean OK if you're
together and everything, you split, whatever . . . The way it is, if
they can get jobs then they go and get drunk or whatever." When
asked if that's why she had not gotten married, she stated,

> I don't think I want to get married but then . . . see you're sup-
> posed to stick to that one and that's a fantasy. You know, stick
> with one for the rest of your life. I've never met many people
> like that, have you? . . . If they're married and have kids. Them
> kids come in and it seems like the men get jealous 'cause you're
> spending your time on them. OK they can get up and go anytime.
> A woman has to stick there all the time 'cause she got them kids
> behind their backs.

Women in the inner city tended to believe that black men got
involved with women mainly to obtain sex or money, and that
once these goals had been achieved, the women were usually dis-
carded. For example, one woman from a poor neighborhood on the
West Side of Chicago was asked if she still saw the father of her
child. She stated, "He left before the baby was born, I was about
two weeks pregnant and he said that he didn't want to be bothered and I said 'Fine—you go your way and I go mine.'" Another
woman—a twenty-one-year-old, part-time–employed, unmarried
mother of two children, and also a resident of a poor neighborhood
on the West Side—voiced this general complaint about men:

Some mens can't speak to one woman. Some man might try to force theyself to do that, then again you really can't believe it so a, a female have to be careful, really careful. She have to learn really if this man really care about her, if he gonna do what he really does, what he say he, what he plan on doing, you know. So, you know—'cause they be out to get one thing, nothing but sex from a female.

There was a widespread feeling among women in the inner city that black males had relationships with more than one female at a time. And since some young men left their girlfriends as soon as they became pregnant, it was not uncommon to find a black male who had fathered at least three children by three separate women. Despite the problematic state of these relationships, sex among inner-city black teenagers was widely practiced. In the ethnographic phase of our research, respondents reported that sex was an integral and expected aspect of their romantic relationships. Males especially felt peer pressure to be sexually active. They said that the members of their peer networks bragged about their sexual encounters and that they felt obligated to reveal their own sexual exploits. Little consideration was given to the implications or consequences of sexual matters for the longer-term relationship or for childbearing. These reports could be loosely construed as evidence for the cool-pose culture among young black men discussed in Chapter 3.

Whereas women blamed men for the poor gender relations, men maintained that it was the women who were troublesome. The men complained that it was not easy to deal with the women's suspicions about their behavior and intentions. They also felt that material resources especially attracted women and that it was therefore difficult to find women who were supportive of partners with a low living standard.

These antagonistic relationships influenced the views of both men and women about marriage. The ethnographic data revealed especially weak support for the institution of marriage in the inner-city ghetto among black men. Many of the men viewed marriage as tying them down and resulting in a loss of freedom. "Marriage. You can't have it, you can't do the things you wanna do then," stated an unemployed twenty-one-year-old unmarried father of one child from a poor neighborhood on the West Side.

> She [the spouse] might want you in at a certain time and all, all this. You can't hang out when you married, you know. You married to be with her . . . I like, you know, spending my time, half the time with my friends and then come in when I want to . . . In my book it [marriage] is something that is bad. Like, like fighting, divorce.

A twenty-seven-year-old unmarried, employed father of one child made a similar point: Marriage "cuts down a lot of things you used to do, like, staying out late, stuff like that, hanging with the fellows all day, like, now you can do what the hell you want to do, now, when you—when you married, got a family, it cuts a lot of that stuff off."

The men in the inner city generally felt that it was much better for all parties to remain in a nonmarital relationship until the relationship dissolved rather than getting married and then having to get a divorce. A twenty-five-year-old unmarried West Side resident, the father of one child, expressed this view:

> Well, most black men feel now, why get married when you got six to seven womens to one guy, really. You know, 'cause there's more women out here mostly than men. 'Cause most dudes around

here are killing each other like fools over drugs or all this other stuff. And if you're not that bad looking of a guy, you know, and you know a lot of women like you, why get married when you can play the field the way they want to do, you know?

A twenty-five-year-old part-time worker with a seven-year-old daughter explained why he had avoided marriage following the child's birth:

For years I have been observing other marriages. They all have been built on the wrong foundation. The husband misuses the family or neglects the family or the wife do the same, ah, they just missing a lot of important elements. I had made a commitment to marry her really out of people pleasing. My mom wanted me to do it; her parents wanted us to do it. Taking their suggestions and opinions about the situation over my own and [I] am a grown man. These decisions is for me to make and I realized that they were going to go to expect it to last for 20, 40 years so I evaluated my feelings and came to the honest conclusion that was not right for me, right. And I made the decision that the baby, that I could be a father without necessarily living there.

Others talk about avoiding or delaying marriage for economic reasons. "It made no sense to just get married because we have a baby like other people . . . do," argued an eighteen-year-old unmarried father of a two-week-old son. "If I couldn't take care of my family, why get married?"

These various responses show that marriage was "not in the forefront of the men's minds."[61] The dominant attitude among the young, single black fathers in our Chicago study was, "I'll get married in the future when I am no longer having fun and when I get a job or a better job."[62] Marriage would limit their ability to date other women or "hang out" with the boys. The ethnographic data clearly reveal that the birth of a child did not create a sense of obligation to marry, and that most young fathers felt little pressure, from either their family or their partner's family, to marry. For young African American men in the inner city, having children and getting married were not usually connected.

There is very little research on changing norms and sanctions regarding the family in the inner city,[63] but the norms do appear to have changed. In a study of fathering in the inner city based on a series of interviews with the same respondents over several years, Frank Furstenberg notes,

> I have no way of knowing for sure, but I think that families now exert less pressure on men to remain involved than they once did. I found no instance, for example, of families urging their children to marry or even to live together as was common when I was studying the parents of my informants in the mid-1960s.[64]

The data from our Chicago study, however, indicate that the young men did "feel some obligation to contribute something to support their children."[65] The level of financial support was low and often erratic, however, varying from occasionally buying disposable diapers to regularly contributing several hundred dollars a month. As Frank Furstenberg points out,

> When ill-timed pregnancies occur in unstable partnerships to men who have few material resources for managing unplanned parenthood, they challenge, to say the least, the commitment of young fathers. Fatherhood occurs to men who often have a personal biography that poorly equips them to act on their intentions, even when their intentions to do for their children are

strongly felt. And fatherhood [in the inner city] takes place in a culture where the gap between good intentions and good performance is large and widely recognized.[66]

Black women in the inner city were more interested in marriage, but their expectations for matrimony were low and they did not hold the men they encountered in very high regard. The women felt that even if they did marry, the marriage was likely to be unsuccessful. They maintained that husbands were not as dedicated to their wives as in previous generations and that they would not be able to depend on their husbands even if they did get married.

A young welfare mother of three children from a high-poverty neighborhood on the West Side of Chicago made the following point:

Well, to my recollection, twenty years ago I was only seven years [old] but . . . twenty years ago, men, if they got a woman pregnant, that if they didn't marry her, they stood by her and took care of the child. And nowadays, when a man makes you pregnant, they're goin' off and leave you and think nothing of it. And also . . . also, uh, twenty years ago, I find that there were more people getting married and when they got married they were staying together. I found that with a lot of couples nowadays, that when they get married they're so quick to get a divorce. I've thought about marriage myself many times, uh, but nowadays, it seems to me that when it comes to marriage, it just doesn't mean anything to people. At least the men that I talk to. And also, twenty years ago, I think families were closer [police siren]. I found now families are drifting apart, they're not as loving as they were twenty years ago. I find with a lot of families now, they're quicker to hurt you than to help you.

A thirty-one-year-old divorcée and welfare mother of four children from a South Side high-poverty neighborhood expressed the view that welfare enables some women to avoid marriage:

> I still say I wouldn't get married. You know, like some people say, there's a lot of elderly people that say, "It's best to get a child a father's name, it's best to do that." But I think that by having public aid, and if you do happen to wind up with a lot of kids, until you're able to get on your feet, it's better not to get married. Because the actual status between an unmarried woman on welfare, and an unmarried man on welfare is a lot different when they have kids or have no kids. If you have kids, you say, "OK, he's going to do it better for me anyway," so we get married, change the names of the kids. And then, "I'm not working, them's not my kids." If you're not married to the person you say, "They're not yours? Hit the door then!" But if you're married to them, you say, "Hit the door, please?" You know, you start nagging and they say, "I'm not going nowhere." So you say, "Well, I'll put you out." But you can't put them out, can't do nothing. You're stuck with them just like all the other people stuck with their marriage and stuff. I think it's best, once you get a family started, and you're not as educated as well as you wanted to be, it's not good to get married. That's one thing I would never do again is get married . . . I think it's best not to get married. Unless you're pretty sure that person's going to take care of you.

Finally, a twenty-seven-year-old single woman (who was childless, had four years of college, worked as a customer service representative, and lived in a high-poverty neighborhood on the South Side) talked about changes in the family structure in relation to her own personal situation. She stated that there had been a definite change in the family structure as far as the mother and father being together.

> The way things are going now you'll find more single women having kids, but not totally dependent on the guy being there. I know there's a change in friends of mine who have kids, the father isn't there with them. They're not so totally dependent on him any more. They're out there doing for themselves . . . You have to make it one way or another, and you can't depend on him to come through or him to be there. And a lot of them are searching for someone to be with, but if [he] comes he does and if he doesn't he doesn't. Because I always say by the time I'm thirty, if I'm not married, I know I'll still have me a child. But I wouldn't be so hung up on the idea of having somebody be there. I probably wouldn't have a child by anyone I was seeing or anything. I'd probably go through a sperm bank. I think financially I could do it, but I would need help as far as babysitting and stuff.

The ethnographic data reveal that both inner-city black males and females believe that since most marriages will eventually break up and no longer represent meaningful relationships, it is better to avoid the entanglements of wedlock altogether. For many single mothers in the inner city, remaining single makes more sense as a family formation strategy than does marriage. Single mothers who perceive the fathers of their children as unreliable or as having limited financial means will often—rationally—choose single parenthood. From the point of view of day-to-day survival, single parenthood reduces the emotional burden and shields these women from the type of exploitation that often accompanies the sharing of both living arrangements and limited resources. Men and women are extremely suspicious of each other, and their concerns range from the degree of financial commitment to fidelity. For all these reasons, women in our study often stated they did not want to get married until they were sure it was going to work out—and by "work out" they meant that they wanted a spouse who would contribute financially and emotionally to them and to their children.

However, these ethnographic findings are based on research conducted in the late 1980s. Although it could be argued that relations between inner-city men and women, including marital relations, could have changed significantly since then, Kathryn Edin and Maria Kefalas presented similar findings in a more recent study. In their book, *Promises I Can Keep: Why Poor Women Put Motherhood before Marriage*, Edin and Kefalas collected and analyzed data on low-income black, white, and Puerto Rican single mothers in Camden, New Jersey (one of America's poorest cities), and in eight poor neighborhoods in Philadelphia.[67]

Edin and Kefalas found that the low-income, young mothers they interviewed valued motherhood highly. Indeed, their identity, emotional fulfillment, personal success, and hope for the future were tied to motherhood. The thought of not being a parent or of postponing parenting until their thirties—a common practice for middle-class women—was anathema to the women in this study. However, the respondents also valued marriage and hoped to be married some day. Edin and Kefalas forcefully argue that poor women postpone marriage not because they value it lightly, but because they feel that they cannot commit to marriage until they are confident of success.

The basic problem they face, as did the women in our earlier Chicago study, is that the men to whom they have access tend not to be marriageable because of a range of problems: poor education, chronic joblessness, low earning, criminal records, spells of incarceration, drug and alcohol abuse, intimate violence, and chronic infidelity. There is a short supply of good, decent, trustworthy men in their world. The better-off men go to the better-off women. It is not surprising that the relationships these women have with the fathers of their children are plagued with physical abuse, mistrust, and infidelity. The women therefore wait until they can find a man they can trust—a man who has, over time, proven himself to be a dependable and responsible partner and father. Their dreams include financial security and having a house before getting married. And because all of these conditions are so difficult to meet, they become mothers long before they become wives, and some never marry.

Edin and Kefalas point out that unlike many affluent women, the poor women they studied do not view having a child out of wedlock as ruining their lives, because they feel that their future would be even bleaker without children. For these women, motherhood is the most important social role they believe they will ever play, and it is the surest accomplishment they can attain. Many of the women told Edin and Kefalas that they had been headed for trouble until they got pregnant and turned their lives around because of a desire to be good mothers. Many of them said that having children had been a life-altering experience and that they could not imagine living without children.

Whereas middle-class women often put off marriage and childbearing to pursue economic goals, poor women have children in the absence of better opportunities. The mothers in this study expressed confidence in their ability to provide for their children. However, because these mothers frequently fail to recognize the disadvantages that will affect their children's chances in life, this confidence is often unjustified. In this sense their cultural framing of marriage and motherhood not only shapes how they respond to poverty—it may also indirectly affect their children's odds of escaping poverty. The implication here is that the decision to forgo or delay marriage increases the odds that the family will live in persistent poverty.

In 1978, sociologist Diana Pearce coined the term "feminization of poverty" to describe the increase of female-headed households among the poor.[68] Since then, studies have repeatedly reported that married-couple families are far less likely to be in poverty than are households headed by a single mother. In one study, whereas only slightly more than 5 percent of married-couple families lived in poverty in 2004, nearly 30 percent of female-headed families were poor.[69] According to another study, "children in single-female-headed households account for more than 60% of all children in families living in poverty."[70] This effect is not unique to any one group. The poverty rate of white children in households headed by single females was almost 5 times greater than the poverty rate for those in married-couple families; for black children the rate was 4.5 times greater, and for Hispanic children it was 2.4 times greater. The author states, "Because of the high rates of poverty experienced by children in families headed by single females, black children in single-female-headed families account for more than 85% of all poor black children."[71] Finally, a longitudinal study that tracked a national random sample of families over several years revealed that poverty tends to be chronic for children in single-mother families where the mother was either never married or was a teenager when the child was born.[72]

It has been argued that because married-couple families frequently have two potential (and often actual) breadwinners, their chances of preventing or escaping poverty are much greater than those of families headed by single females.[73] Given the extremely high jobless rate among low-skilled black males, however, this argument—although generally true—is less applicable to poor black families in the inner city.

The Interaction of Culture and Social Structure

Edin and Kefalas's study provides a compelling argument for examining the role of culture under conditions of chronic economic hardship and its impact on family life. And the finding of similar views on motherhood and marriage that they uncovered among poor women from different groups (African Americans, Puerto Ricans, and whites) reinforce Lamont and Small's argument on meaning making—namely, that our focus for study should be on cultural frames that develop in different spatial and contextual circumstances, and how they orient action, rather than on the shared values of members of a particular racial or ethnic group.

Nonetheless, by one logic, every woman in Edin and Kefalas's study—black, white, or Puerto Rican—was likely to respond to urban poverty by finding positive meaning in having out-of-wedlock children. By a different logic, the unique historical racial experiences of inner-city blacks may have also influenced their cultural framing of marriage and motherhood in ways not captured by Edin and Kefalas.[74] I tend to think that both logics apply—that is, that all the women in this study could find meaning and purpose in child rearing in spite of serious financial hardship, and that black women would, on balance, have particular views on family formed through the unique circumstances tied to the racial segregation. However, I would place far more weight on the former because it reveals that not only blacks, but other ethnic groups, have responded to conditions of poverty in similar ways. How families are formed among America's poorest citizens is an area that cries out for further research.

Changing patterns of family formation are not limited to the inner-city black community but are part of wider societal trends.

The commitment to traditional husband–wife families and the stigma associated with out-of-wedlock births, separation, and divorce have waned significantly in the United States. "The labor market conditions which sustained the 'male breadwinner' family have all but vanished."[75] This shift has gradually led to the creation of a new set of orientations that place less value on marriage and reject the dominance of men as a standard for a successful nuclear family.[76]

Like all other groups, inner-city blacks are influenced by these norms. But they also have unique experiences that derive from decades of racial segregation and highly concentrated poverty that reinforce these norms. The same argument applies when I compare the findings in our Chicago study with those of Edin and Kefalas. More specifically, just as the white, Puerto Rican, and black mothers in their study emphasized the loss of personal freedom, fear about the lack of dedication a partner might feel toward them, and the importance of having secure jobs and financial security before seriously considering matrimony, so too did the inner-city blacks in our Chicago study. Moreover, just as the mothers in the Edin and Kefalas study saw little reason to contemplate seriously the consequences of single parenthood, because their prospects for social and economic mobility were severely limited whether they were married or not, so too did the inner-city blacks in our Chicago study. But the comparisons should not stop here.

My concern about the Edin and Kefalas study is that their emphasis on commonalities obscured any differences that might exist among poor black, Puerto Rican, and white mothers. In other words, they neglected to explore any differences that might stem from racial experiences. I am not referring to racial experiences that go back to slavery, as argued in the speculative cultural continuity thesis, but experiences in the context of living in racially segregated ghettos where problems of poverty, joblessness, and lack of opportunity are exacerbated by the cumulative problems of race.

Nonetheless, as suggested by the title of this book and in the material covered thus far, the experiences of poor, inner-city blacks represent the influences of more than just race. Their responses to marriage and childbearing also stem from the linkage between new structural realities, changing norms, and evolving cultural patterns. The new structural realities may be seen in the diminishing employment opportunities for low-skilled workers. The decline of the mass production system and the rise of new jobs in the highly technological global economy that require training and education have severely weakened the labor force attachment among inner-city workers. As employment prospects recede, the foundation for stable relationships becomes weaker over time. More permanent relationships such as marriage give way to temporary liaisons that result in broken relationships, out-of-wedlock pregnancies and births, and, in the rare occurrence of marriage, to separation and divorce. The changing norms for marriage in the larger society also reinforce the movement toward temporary liaisons in the inner city, and therefore economic considerations in marital decisions take on even greater significance.

Conclusion

In previous chapters I argued that the available evidence suggests that structural factors are more important than cultural variables in accounting for concentrated poverty in the inner city and the economic and social position of poor black males. As revealed in this chapter, the structural evidence for the fragmentation of poor black families is not as compelling. Our study of family life and poverty in Chicago provided retrospective data revealing that marriage had declined much more sharply among young, jobless African American fathers than among young, employed black fathers. However, the findings from national research on the relationship of both employment and earnings to rates of marriage are mixed—showing a strong relationship at a single point in time, but a weak association over a period of time.

Nonetheless, the research on African American families discussed in this chapter provides little reason to conclude that cultural variables have played a greater role than structural factors in black family fragmentation. Indeed, the available data suggest the opposite conclusion. The evidence to corroborate the cultural continuity thesis is insufficient. Furthermore, research reveals that the cultural responses among poor women—black, white, and Puerto Rican—tend to be similar. In the absence of definitive evidence, we can only speculate whether the historic racial experiences of inner-city African American women have uniquely influenced their cultural framing of marriage and motherhood.

We can confidently state, however, that regardless of the relative significance of structural and cultural factors in black family fragmentation, they interact in ways far too important for social scientists and policy makers to ignore.

CHAPTER 5

FRAMING THE ISSUES: UNITING STRUCTURE AND CULTURE

In some of my earlier writings I tended to discuss culture as if it were solely a by-product of structural forces.[1] One scholar who has been critical of this approach is Loïc Wacquant, who argues that it "guts out the symbolic dimension of social life in the ghetto. It robs culture of any autonomy."[2] This book addresses this criticism. We have seen that some cultural patterns in the inner-city ghetto reflect informal rules that shape how people interact or engage one another and make decisions. The decision making is often related to perceptions about how the world works—what we call meaning making. The meaning-making and decision-making processes evolve over time in situations imposed by racial segregation and poverty, situations that severely hamper social mobility. To state this process in formal sociological terms, culture *mediates* the impact of structural forces such as racial segregation and poverty. In other words, residents of the ghetto develop ways, often quite creative, to adjust and respond to chronic racial and economic subordination, as reflected in meaning-making and decision-making processes, including those resulting in the development of informal codes that regulate behavior.

Sociologists have provided detailed descriptions of such cultural codes in inner-city ghetto neighborhoods. Two prominent examples were discussed in Chapter 1: the "code of the street" and the "code of shady dealings." The former represents an informal but explicit set of rules that have evolved to regulate violence and govern interpersonal public behavior in neighborhoods with high crime and low police protection.[3] The latter represents an informal but explicit set of rules that regulate off-the-books trading in the underground economy, rules that stipulate what is expected of individuals involved in these exchanges and where the transactions should take place.[4] Even though these codes emerge under conditions of poverty and racial segregation, once developed they display a degree of autonomy in the regulation of behavior. The behavior generated by these autonomous cultural forces often reinforces the very conditions that have emerged from structural inequities. For example, deep involvement in the code of the street and the code of shady dealings ultimately reduces one's chances for successful integration into the broader society and thereby contributes to the perpetuation of poverty. As sociologist Deirdre Bloome appropriately puts it, "at any one moment both cultural and current structural forces work to shape future cultural and structural circumstances; the interplay is like a chain of cumulative causation."[5]

As the longitudinal articles on intergenerational transmission and durable effects of concentrated neighborhood poverty discussed in Chapter 2 reveal, when we take time into account we see that the causal flow between structure and culture becomes more complex.[6] The integration of temporality in our analysis helps dissolve the strict structure–culture distinction: depending on *when* we look at a social process, we will see that the relationship between structure and culture may flow in a different direction. For example, as the earlier discussion of cultural codes—the code of the street and the code of shady dealings—indicated, structure influences culture as seen in the emergence of these codes, and these cultural codes in turn influence structure in the sense of perpetuating poverty. When we go beyond cross-sectional analysis (an analysis that focuses on only a specific point in time), we are more likely to develop a picture of social reality and the interaction between structure and culture that is far more complex and sophisticated.[7]

Nonetheless, as I have argued in this book, more weight should be given to structural causes of inequality, despite the dynamic interrelationships of structure and culture, because they continue to play a far greater role in the subjugation of black Americans and other people of color. In addition, culture is less causally autonomous than social structure in the sense that it more often plays a mediating role in determining African Americans' chances in life, as described earlier.

Policy makers who are dedicated to combating the problems of race and poverty and who recognize the importance of structural inequities face two challenges. First is the problem of *institutional entrenchment*, which always reduces the chances of reform. For example, as Bloome says, "we cannot expect equity in [public] school funding, much less the disproportionate allocation of resources to the most needy, without changing long-accepted mechanisms for allocating resources and staffing, which have become 'normal' and gained constituencies willing to fight to maintain their current privileges."[8] And overcoming institutional entrenchment should be one of our primary objectives if we are committed to combating inequality.

The second challenge facing policy makers committed to reform is how to generate political support from Americans, who tend to place far more emphasis on cultural factors and individual behavior than on structural inequities in explaining social and economic outcomes. After all, beliefs that attribute joblessness and poverty to individual shortcomings do not engender strong support for social programs to end inequality. But in addressing the problem of structural inequities, it would not be wise to leave the impression in public discussions that cultural problems do not matter. Indeed, proposals to address racial inequality should reflect awareness of the inextricable link between aspects of structure and culture.

The ongoing social science debate over the role of social structure versus culture in shaping the social outcomes of African Americans has apparently done little to educate Americans on the importance of a relationship between structural inequities and culture. As we have seen, ideological inclinations often predict what position is taken. Whereas liberals tend to focus on structural conditions, especially racialist structural factors such as segregation and discrimination, conservatives tend to emphasize cultural factors such as individual attitudes and behavior.

Over the years I have reflected on this debate. However, not until I attended a panel discussion at the University of Chicago in 1995 on Richard J. Herrnstein and Charles Murray's controversial book *The Bell Curve: Intelligence and Class in American Life*,[9] did I see the most compelling reason for *combining* cultural arguments with structural arguments. Integration of the two could be used to construct a truly comprehensive explanation of the social and economic outcomes of poor people of color and provide more compelling arguments for those policy makers who are truly committed to eradicating racial inequality in our society, where a majority of citizens believe that personal, not structural, factors account for differences in social and economic achievements.

In *The Bell Curve*, Herrnstein and Murray found differences in the test scores of blacks and whites even after they included social environmental factors such as family education, father's occupation, and household income in their analyses. They used this difference in test scores to support the argument that the social and economic outcomes of blacks and whites differ at least in part because of genetic endowment—a position suggesting that African Americans are innately inferior. To my mind, none of the panelists gathered that day at the University of Chicago provided a satisfactory rebuttal. And I left the discussion thinking that Herrnstein and Murray's argument for the importance of group differences in cognitive ability was based on an incredibly weak measure of the social environment. In other words, simply controlling for differences in family education, father's occupation, and household income hardly captures differences in cumulative environmental experiences. Herrnstein and Murray did not provide measures of the cumulative and durable effects of race, including the effects of prolonged residence in racially segregated neighborhoods.

The two recent groundbreaking longitudinal studies described in Chapter 2 show that these cumulative effects are both structural and cultural, and they had not been adequately captured in the quantitative research on race and poverty that dominated debates at the time *The Bell Curve* was published.[10] Paradoxically, although liberal social scientists rejected the book's "inferiority thesis," in effect they were playing into the hands of Herrnstein and Murray by not conducting research that would illuminate all the dimensions of the social environment. By ignoring the impact of culture and how it interacts with structural forces, they were not able to capture all the important features of the social environment.

If culture is the sharing of outlooks and modes of behavior that are sustained through social interaction within a community and often transmitted from generation to generation, then patterns of behavior in racially segregated inner-city neighborhoods often represent particular cultural traits that emanate from or are the products of racial exclusion.[11] As noted in previous chapters, some of these traits may impede successful maneuvering in the larger society. Accordingly, to fully explain or understand the divergent social and economic outcomes of racial groups, we must take cultural influences in the environment into account.

For all of these reasons, it is extremely important to discuss how the issues of race and poverty are framed in public policy discussions. How we situate social issues in the larger context of society says a lot about our commitment to change. A useful example of how this works comes to me from Robert Asen, a professor in the Department of Communication Arts at the University of Wisconsin. He reminded me that the *political framing* of poverty—that is, the way political leaders formulate arguments about how we as a nation should talk about and address issues of poverty—in the New Deal era was quite different from the political framing of poverty in our own times.

During the New Deal era the emphasis was on structure—namely, the devastating impact of the economic crisis. Americans clearly recognized that hundreds of thousands of citizens were poor or unemployed mainly because of a severe and prolonged job shortage. In the public arena today, poverty tends to be discussed in reference to individual initiative. This distinction, he points out, reveals how larger shifts in society have influenced our understanding of the nature of poverty. Therefore, we ought to consider the contingency of political frames at particular moments in time. These "deliberative frames" not only orient our debates on public policy, but they can also be shifted through debate. So, just because cultural explanations resonate with policy makers and the public today does not mean that structural explanations cannot resonate with them tomorrow. To shift political frames, however, and hopefully provide a more balanced discussion, requires parallel efforts among politicians, engaged citizens, and scholars.[12]

Sociological research provides some examples of how political frames might be shifted to address racial inequities—not in a cynical way to manipulate public opinion, but to make a true case for needed political and social reform. In 1990, almost seven in ten white Americans opposed quotas to admit black students in colleges and universities and more than eight in ten objected to the idea of preferential hiring and promotion of blacks. However, research suggests that such strong white opposition to quotas and preferential hiring and promotion should not lead us to overlook the fact that some affirmative action policies are supported by wide segments of the white population, regardless of racial attitudes.

As the Harvard sociologist Lawrence Bobo points out, the view that white opposition to affirmative action is monolithic is distorted: "Affirmative action policies span a range of policy goals and strategies. Some formulations of which (e.g., race-targeted scholarships or special job outreach and training efforts) can be quite popular."[13] For example, recent studies reveal that although they oppose the "preferential" racial policies associated with quotas or job hiring and promotion strategies designed to achieve equal outcomes, most white Americans approve of "opportunity-enhancing" affirmative action policies, such as race-targeted programs for job training, education, and recruitment. In the 1990 General Social Survey, 68 percent of all whites favored spending more money on the schools in black neighborhoods, especially for early education

programs. And 70 percent favored granting special college scholarships to black children who maintain good grades.[14] In their
large survey of households in the Boston metropolitan area, Barry
Bluestone and Mary Huff Stevenson found that, whereas only
18 percent of the white male and 13 percent of the white female
respondents favored or strongly favored job *preferences* for blacks,
59 percent of the white males and 70 percent of the white females
favored or strongly favored special job training and education for
blacks.[15]

Accordingly, programs that enable blacks to take advantage of
opportunities are less likely to be "perceived as challenging the
values of individualism and the work ethic."[16] The implications for
political framing are obvious—opportunity-enhancing affirmative
action programs are supported because they reinforce the belief
that the allocation of jobs and economic rewards should be based
on individual effort, training, and talent.

Ronald Haskins, a policy analyst at the Brookings Institution,
suggests a shift in framing to aid the working poor. He argues that
a way to frame policy issues today would be to emphasize personal
responsibility with government support. He notes that bipartisan
support for working families increased in Congress following passage of the 1996 welfare reform legislation. Haskins notes that the
slogan "people who are working should not be poor" resonated with
those on Capitol Hill and led to increased support for child care,
the State Children's Health Insurance Program (SCHIP), child
tax credits, Medicaid, and the Earned Income Tax Credit (EITC)
in the years immediately following passage of the 1996 welfare
reform bill.[17]

Still, much of welfare reform debate in the Republican-
controlled Congress prior to the legislation of 1996—which was
framed narrowly in terms of individual factors and cultural expla-

nations (not structural explanations such as those that highlight the impact of joblessness)—influenced the enactment of welfare legislation. For example, one of the most widely discussed policies associated with the welfare reform bill was the marriage promotion legislation, which focuses solely on cultural factors—that is, changing the attitudes and behavior of individuals. The challenge facing those of us who seek to change outcomes for the poor and the marginalized is to frame the issues so that the American public comes to recognize that structural inequities are the most powerful forces shaping individual and family responses, and that cultural programs, although desirable, should be combined with strong efforts to attack structural inequities.

In my previous writings I called for the framing of issues designed to appeal to broad segments of the population.[18] Key to this framing, I argued, would be an emphasis on policies that would directly benefit all groups, not just people of color. My thinking was that, given American views about poverty and race, a color-blind agenda would be the most realistic way to generate the broad political support necessary to enact the required legislation. I no longer hold to this view.

The question is not whether the policy should be race-neutral or universal; the question is whether the policy is framed to facilitate a frank discussion of the problems that ought to be addressed and to generate broad political support to alleviate them. So now my position has changed: in framing public policy we should not shy away from an explicit discussion of the specific issues of race and poverty; on the contrary, we should highlight them in our attempt to convince the nation that these problems should be seriously confronted and that there is an urgent need to address them. The issues of race and poverty should be framed in such a way that not only is a sense of fairness and justice to combat inequality generated, but also people are made aware that our country would be better off if these problems were seriously addressed and eradicated.

In considering this change of frame—indeed, a change of mind-set on race and poverty—I am drawn to then-Senator Barack Obama's speech on race given March 18, 2008. His oratory provides a model for the type of framing I have in mind.[19] In taking on the tough topic of race in America, Obama spoke to the issue of structure and culture, as well as their interaction. He drew America's attention to the many disparities that exist between the "African-American community and the larger American community today"—disparities that "can be traced to inequalities passed on from an earlier generation that suffered under the brutal legacy of slavery and Jim Crow." He also discussed the lack of economic opportunity among black men, and how "the shame and frustration that came from not being able to provide for one's family contributed to the erosion of black families." Obama called on whites to acknowledge that

> the path to a more perfect union means acknowledging that what ails the African-American community does not just exist in the minds of black people; that the legacy of discrimination—and current incidents of discrimination, while less overt than in the past—are real and must be addressed, not just with words, but with deeds, by investing in our schools and our communities; by enforcing our civil rights laws and ensuring fairness in our criminal justice system; by providing this generation with ladders of opportunity that were unavailable for previous generations. It requires all Americans to realize that your dreams do not have to come at the expense of my dreams; that investing in the health, welfare and education of black and brown and white children will ultimately help all of America prosper.

However, Obama did not restrict his speech to addressing structural inequities; he also focused on problematic cultural and behavioral responses to these inequities, including a cycle of violence among black men and a "legacy of defeat" that has been passed on to future generations. And he urged those in the African American community to take full responsibility for their lives by demanding more from their fathers, and by spending more time with their children "reading to them, and teaching them that while they may face challenges and discrimination in their own lives, they must never succumb to despair or cynicism; they must always believe that they can write their own destiny."

By combining a powerful discussion of structural inequities with an emphasis on personal responsibility, Obama did not isolate the latter from the former, as is so often the case in the remarks of talk show hosts, journalists, and conservative politicians and commentators. His speech gave an honest appraisal of structural racial inequality as he called for all Americans to support blacks in their struggle to help themselves. As I think back on my discussion of white support for opportunity-enhancing affirmative action programs and the congressional support for programs to help the working poor during the first term of the George W. Bush administration, I feel that the perspective offered in Obama's speech is exactly the type of framing that can result in broad support to address the problems of race and poverty.

The Background Case for a New Framing

In this book I advocate for a framework for understanding the formation and maintenance of racial inequality that integrates cultural factors with two types of structural forces: those that directly reflect explicit racial bias and those that do not. I mapped this framework onto three areas that have generated particularly intense debates among the proponents of cultural and structural explanations of social outcomes in the black community: changes in the inner-city ghetto, the predicament of low-skilled black males, and the weakening of the black family. In the process of considering the available evidence in each of these three areas, it becomes clear to me that we need to tease out the complex interplay of structural and cultural factors as they influence the lives of poor black Americans.

STRUCTURAL FORCES

Although I discuss racialist structural factors that have contributed directly and visibly to racial inequality, the most important point of this book is to draw attention to issues that have not traditionally been the focus of studies on race and urban poverty, because they have contributed *indirectly* to racial inequality. Primary among these are government policies or decisions that, upon superficial examination, seem nonracial—that is, not motivated solely to control or exclude persons by race. Nevertheless, the following actions on behalf of the "public welfare" had—and, I would argue, continue to have—a profound impact on inner-city neighborhoods and their poor black residents:

- Federal transportation and highway policy shifted jobs from the cities to the suburbs.
- Mortgage-interest tax exemptions and mortgages for veterans jointly facilitated the out-migration of working- and middle-class families from inner-city neighborhoods, leaving blacks isolated in central cities.

- Urban renewal and the building of freeway and highway networks destroyed the pedestrian patterns and economic logic of many stable, low-income, black neighborhoods.
- The New Federalists' fiscal policies resulted in drastic cuts in federal aid to cities whose populations had become more black and brown.
- Weak labor market policies, which led to a sharp reduction in the real value of the minimum wage, and regressive tax policies combined to undermine the ability of poor, inner-city workers to support their families.

In this book I also discuss complex economic transformations that do not reflect actions, processes, or ideologies that explicitly denote racial bias, but that nonetheless have profoundly affected poor African American communities. These include the decreased relative demand for low-skilled labor caused by the technological revolution and the growing internationalization of economic activity; the relocation of urban industries first to suburbs and then to points overseas for a sharp decline in the central-city manufacturing sector; and urban sprawl that reduces inner-city residents' access to economic opportunities and exacerbates the "spatial mismatch" between poor black neighborhoods and jobs that pay well.

Although all American workers have been struggling with the changing landscape of jobs in this country, the decline in locally situated industrial employment has been especially devastating to inner-city neighborhoods. The departure of jobs from the cities coincided with the end of the Second Great Migration of poor blacks from the rural South to the urban North around 1970. Suddenly, many poor black communities, especially those in the Northeast and Midwest, went from being densely packed neighborhoods of recently arrived migrants to areas gradually abandoned by nonpoor residents who, because of their greater social and economic resources, had contributed over the years to neighborhood stability. This out-migration not only resulted in depopulation, because the ranks of those who left were not replaced with incoming migrants, but it also increased the proportion of remaining residents who are poor, resulting in what sociologists call greater concentrations of poverty.[20]

Several indirect structural factors have contributed to the incredibly high jobless rate of low-skilled black males and their correspondingly low incomes, some of which are familiar from the list just provided. These include the decreased relative demand for low-skilled labor caused by the computer revolution, the growing internationalization of economic activity, the decline of the manufacturing sector, and the growth of service industries where most of the new jobs for workers with limited education and training are concentrated. And, of course, the shift to service industries has been especially problematic for low-skilled black males because the jobs it generates call for workers who can effectively provide personal service and relate to consumers. Employers clearly prefer to hire women for these jobs. And when men are successful in securing service sector work, they tend to be recent immigrants rather than inner-city blacks. African American men, especially those with prison records, do not inspire confidence among employers for service sector jobs.

Finally, indirect structural factors have contributed to fragmentation of the African American family. Contrary to what many Americans believe, there is little evidence to support the view that welfare is a leading contributor to the increase of out-of-wedlock births and solo-parent families in the poor, urban black community. Research conducted before enactment of the 1996 welfare reform act found no relationship between the generosity of benefits and the likelihood that African American girls and women would have children outside of marriage.

Of course, joblessness among black males—which I argue is largely an outcome of the structural factors already listed—come into play in explanations of black family fragmentation. It seems evident to most observers that there is clearly an association between black male joblessness and the rise of single-parent families. Although empirical studies utilizing national data have shown only modest support for the hypothesis linking the sharp increase in poor, black, single-parent families to the declining economic status of young black men, my group's study of family life and poverty in Chicago's inner city in the 1990s revealed that marriage rates declined much more sharply among young, jobless black fathers than among young, employed black fathers.

In all of the indirect structural circumstances described here and discussed at length in the previous chapters, the hand of racial prejudice is not readily visible. Yet, African Americans suffer disproportionately from the effects of these circumstances. Being disadvantaged and pushed to the lower margins of society, poor blacks have few resources for combating these structural factors.

CULTURAL FORCES

Two types of cultural forces contribute to racial inequality: (1) belief systems of the broader society that either explicitly or implicitly give rise to racial inequality and (2) cultural traits that emerge from patterns of intragroup interaction in settings created by racial segregation and discrimination. The former type includes widespread racist beliefs and prejudiced attitudes that have, over the years, reinforced racial disadvantage, including years of Jim Crow segregation before it was eradicated by the series of civil rights laws that began in 1954 with *Brown v. Board of Education*.[21] The latter type refers to shared outlooks, traditions, belief systems, worldviews, preferences, manners, linguistic patterns, clothing styles, and modes of behavior in the inner-city ghetto. These traits are embodied in the micro-level processes of meaning making and decision making—that is, the way individuals in segregated communities develop an understanding of how the world works and make decisions and choices that reflect that understanding.

Social scientists, especially liberal social scientists, have paid little attention to the cultural forces within the inner city that have reinforced poverty and racial inequality. Part of this neglect is ideological. In the aftermath of the controversy over the Moynihan report, liberal social scientists have been reluctant to advance any explanation that invokes a group's cultural attributes. Accordingly, there has been a strong tendency among liberals to rely on structural factors like discrimination, segregation, joblessness, and failing schools. As the sociologist Orlando Patterson points out, avoiding the use of cultural explanations has its origins in a marked reluctance to be perceived as blaming the victim— that, rather than the social environment, the poor themselves are responsible for their own poverty and negative outcomes.[22]

A number of studies have raised questions about the extent to which living in poor neighborhoods affects social and economic outcomes. The most widely discussed of these involve the Moving to Opportunity (MTO) experiment, a program that compared a random sample of residents who had received vouchers to move from high-poverty to low-poverty neighborhoods with a randomly assigned control group of residents that had not received vouchers to move.

Two groundbreaking studies reported in Chapter 2 raised serious questions about the extent to which the MTO captured neighborhood effects.[23] What's more, this work provided compelling evidence that we need to consider the cumulative and sometimes durable effects of residing in poor segregated neighborhoods, including the prolonged structural effects ranging from proximity to jobs to enrollment in low-quality schools, as well as repeated exposure to cultural traits that emanate from or are the products of racial exclusion (e.g., the impact of a child's peer group norms). These two important studies provide direction for much-needed further research on the cumulative effects of living in poor, segregated neighborhoods.

In Chapter 3, cultural arguments that might explain the social outcomes of young black males were closely examined, including the evolution of cool-pose culture, with its emphasis on appearance and fashion, sexual conquests, and partying; the subculture of defeatism, in which individuals give up looking for work because they feel the odds are stacked against them; and the subculture of resistance, in which individuals reject working in low-skilled and menial jobs because they feel those jobs are undignified or beneath them. I noted that the evidence for these cultural arguments is mixed at best, including the evidence for a subculture of resistance. For example, I pointed out that despite the popular view that young, low-skilled black males resist seeking low-wage jobs, the most definitive empirical evidence reveals that black men at the bottom of the income distribution reported lower reservation wages (wages that workers are willing to accept for certain types of work) than did comparable white men. Furthermore, the reported reservation wages of these same black men do not have a significant impact on the duration of their joblessness.

The most compelling evidence for the influence of culture on black men and jobs comes from what Sandra Smith calls a culture of distrust and a discourse of individualism in the low-income black community.[24] She found that the informal job network—those word-of-mouth tips that friends and family pass along to help members of the circle find and keep employment—was particularly weak among low-income blacks. People were hesitant to recommend their friends and family members for jobs. On the one hand, job holders with the information on emerging opportunities justified denying assistance to their relatives and friends, claiming that these persons lacked individual responsibility and motivation. On the other hand, many low-skilled job seekers, particularly black men, are aware of how they are perceived by others in their social environment. And because they are concerned about being demeaned for their joblessness, they hesitate to approach their peers for referrals.

Because employers in low-skilled labor markets heavily rely on personal referrals, this "go it alone" approach proves enormously self-defeating. Here we see how cultural frames, developed from the micro-level processes of meaning making and decision making, orient action—in this case, the limited use of job referrals. The chronic poverty and exploitation in poor black neighborhoods tend to feed inclinations to distrust, thereby undermining the development of cooperative relationships that facilitate the job-matching process.[25]

Perhaps the most contentious debate concerning the role of culture in black social outcomes has focused on black family fragmentation. And much of it has focused on the Moynihan report on the black family, including assertions that the controversy over the report has resulted in a lack of attention to possible *cultural continuities* in the African American family that may be traceable back to slavery. After discussing two notable empirical studies suggesting that black family fragmentation might be an important legacy of slavery and sub-Saharan African family patterns, I expressed support for further exploration of the idea of cultural continuity, even though I remain skeptical about its real impact on the current African American family structure.

If one of the legacies of these sub-Saharan African patterns is that strong ties and obligations to extended kin have led to a greater acceptance of marital separation, that tendency to be apart may become even more pronounced during difficult economic times. But it should be emphasized that currently no evidence supports this speculation. This is not because definitive studies have rejected this idea, but because the issue has yet to be addressed with careful empirical research.

Of course, some scholars question the idea that racial or ethnic groups "have" a culture that most members of the group share, because differences within a group are often as large or even larger than the differences between distinct groups. Some support for this idea was provided in recent research by Kathryn Edin and Maria Kefalas, whose findings on the intimate and fractious relations between men and poor African American, Puerto Rican, and white women were quite similar to the findings my own research group uncovered on the relations between poor black men and women in Chicago's inner cities. Moreover, Edin and Kefalas found similar views on motherhood and marriage among poor African Americans, Puerto Ricans, and white women. The women of all three groups found positive meaning in having children out of wedlock.[26]

In considering this thesis, it seems reasonable to assume that from one point of view, every woman in Edin and Kefalas's study, regardless of race, was likely to respond to conditions of urban poverty by finding positive meaning in having children born out of wedlock. However, one could also argue that the cumulative racial experiences of African Americans may have also influenced their cultural framing of motherhood and marriage in ways that were not captured by Edin and Kefalas's study. I tend to think that both arguments apply; that is, all poor women could find meaning and purpose in child rearing despite serious financial hardship, and African American women have, on balance, formed particular views on family through unique circumstances tied to their experiences with racial oppression in America. I would place far more weight on the former, however, because research clearly reveals that not only African Americans, but also other ethnic groups, have responded in similar ways to conditions of urban poverty. How America's poorest citizens experience and maintain their families is an area that cries out for further research, especially ethnographic research.

Structure and Culture Entwined

As this book unfolded, I laid the groundwork for understanding how structural and cultural forces interact to create racial group outcomes. Nonetheless, a fundamental question remains: what is the relative importance of each of these two dimensions in accounting for the formation and persistence of the inner-city ghetto, the plight of black males, and the breakdown of the black family? Culture matters, but I would have to say it does not matter nearly as much as social structure. Culture is less causally autonomous than social structure, more often playing a mediating role in determining individuals' life outcomes. Emphasizing this point is important because, as argued in Chapter 2, a social scientist who incorporates culture in a comprehensive framework on race and urban poverty has an obligation to highlight the powerful impact of structural forces because cultural explanations are more likely to resonate with the general public and policy makers.

From a historical perspective, it is hard to overstate the importance of racialist structural factors. Aside from the enduring effects of slavery, Jim Crow segregation, public school segregation, legalized discrimination, residential segregation, the FHA's redlining of black neighborhoods in the 1940s and '50s, the construction of public housing projects in poor black neighborhoods, employer discrimination, and other racial acts and processes, there is the impact of political, economic, and policy decisions that were at least partly influenced by race. In contrasting the combined impact of the structural factors with cultural factors, it would be very hard to argue that the cultural factors in the black community are equally as important in determining life chances or creating racial group outcomes. For example, if one attempts to explain rapid changes in social and economic outcomes in the inner city, there is little evidence that cultural forces have the power that changes in the economy have. We need only consider the impact of the economic boom on the reduction of concentrated racial poverty in the 1990s, as discussed in Chapter 2, to illustrate this point.

That said, as this book makes clear, one cannot draw a simple dichotomy between culture and structure in an investigation of their relative impact. They are not mutually exclusive; in fact, they often work in concert. For example, one could argue that national cultural forces as embodied in the various forms of racist attitudes have had a greater impact on the social outcomes of poor African Americans over the years than have the cultural forces within the ghetto. However, racist attitudes are not simply traits of individuals; they are also embedded in social structures. Indeed, as an aspect of culture, racist attitudes gain their power mainly through incorporation into social structures.[27] The most extreme example since the end of slavery, of course, was the embodiment of racist attitudes in Jim Crow segregation, including black disenfranchisement, separate and inferior schools, and circumscribed employment in the low-wage sector. However, as discussed in Chapter 1, the more recent form of racist sentiment, "laissez faire racism"—a view that African Americans are responsible for their own economic predicament and therefore not worthy of special government support—may very well be embodied in the lack of government action to address the problems of race and poverty in America.[28]

This book also argues that culture is not simply a product of structure with no independent or autonomous power. Although cultural forces are often generated, fostered, and empowered by structures, in some cases structures are created or reinforced by cultural forces. For example, as Bruce Western so clearly shows, the changes in the criminal justice system that led to the mass imprisonment of African American males in recent decades were by-products of the cultural reframing of crime punishment driven by conservative political ideology.[29] And, as described in Chapter 3, the weakening of the informal job information network in the inner-city ghetto has been partly a function of an inclination to distrust in the inner city—an inclination that inhibits cooperative relationships needed in the job-matching process.

Conclusion

I return now to the points I made in opening this chapter. Policy makers committed to seriously addressing the problems of race and poverty face two serious challenges: how to create legislation that is designed to confront structural and cultural forces that create and reinforce racial inequality; and how to get sufficient support from the American public to support such legislation. That is why I emphasized the importance of careful political framing of the issues of race and poverty to help accomplish these goals. And I highlighted Barack Obama's important 2008 speech on race because I feel that it is a model for this type of framing.

I conclude now with a strong call for similar hopeful and

positive, candid and critical national framings for our discussions about race and poverty in America. I believe that such framing is necessary to generate and sustain broad political support for comprehensive programs to address both the structural and cultural forces of inequality. By speaking in such frank and hopeful terms, I believe we will be able to construct the common ground that we so urgently need to begin erasing the legacies of historic racial subjugation.

NOTES

CHAPTER 1.

1. Jeffrey C. Alexander and Kenneth Thompson, *A Contemporary Introduction to Sociology: Culture and Society in Transition* (Saint Paul, MN: Paradigm, 2008).

2. Ulf Hannerz, *Soulside: Inquiries into Ghetto Culture and Community* (New York: Columbia University Press, 1991).

3. I first discussed the concepts of indirect and direct forces of racial inequality in my contribution to a coauthored introduction to volume 1 of *America Becoming: Racial Trends and Their Consequences*, eds. Neil J. Smelser, William Julius Wilson, and Faith Mitchell (Washington, DC: National Academy Press, 2001), 1–20.

4. Vivian Henderson, "Race, Economics, and Public Policy," *Crisis* 83 (Fall 1975), 50–55.

5. Ray Marshall, "School-to-Work Processes in the United States" (paper, Carnegie Corporation/Johann Jacobs Foundation, Marbach Castle, Germany, November 3–5, 1994).

6. Based on an analysis of microdata—the Integrated Public Use Microdata Series (IPUMS)—from the Current Population Survey (1962, 1970, 1980, 1990), as well as published data in US Bureau of Labor Statistics, *Employment and Earnings* 48, no. 1 (2001), and 54, no. 1 (2007).

7. Sylvia Nasar, "The Men in Prime of Life Spend Less Time Working," *New York Times*, December 1, 1994; and Stephen J. Rose, *On Shaky Ground: Rising Fears about Incomes and Earnings*, Research Report No. 94-02 (Washington, DC: National Commission for Employment Policy, October 1994).

8. US Bureau of the Census, *Computer Use in the United States: October 1984*, Current Population Reports, Series P-23, no. 155 (Washington, DC: Government Printing Office, 1988), table 4; and US Bureau of the Census, *Computer Use in the United States: 2003*, Current Population Reports, Series P-23, no. 208 (Washington, DC: Government Printing Office, 2003), table D.

9. Alan B. Krueger, "How Computers Have Changed the Wage Structure: Evidence

from Micro Data, 1984–1989," *Quarterly Journal of Economics*, February 1993, 32–60.

10. Alan B. Krueger, *What's Up with Wages?* (Princeton, NJ: Mimeo, Industrial Relations Section, Princeton University, 1997); Lawrence Katz, *Wage Subsidies for the Disadvantaged*, NBER Working Paper No. 5679 (Cambridge, MA: National Bureau of Economic Research, 1996); and David Schwartzman, *Black Unemployment: Part of Unskilled Unemployment* (Westport, CT: Greenwood Press, 1997).

11. Schwartzman, *Black Unemployment*.

12. James K. Galbraith, *Created Unequal: The Crisis in American Pay* (New York: Free Press, 1998), 9.

13. Schwartzman, *Black Unemployment*. Alan Krueger remarks, "Whatever the role that trade has played in the past, I suspect that trade will place greater pressure on low-skilled workers in the future. The reason for this suspicion is simply that there are a great many unskilled workers in the world who are paid very little. One and a half billion potential workers have left schools before they reach age 13; half the world's workers leave at age 16 or earlier. When these workers are brought into global economic competition (because of greater openness, more political stability, and greater investment in developing countries), the consequences are unlikely to be positive for low-skilled workers in developed countries." Krueger, *What's Up with Wages?*

14. See Stanley Lieberson, *A Piece of the Pie: Black and White Immigrants since 1880* (Berkeley: University of California Press, 1980); and Kathryn Neckerman, *Schools Betrayed: Roots of Failure in Inner-City Education* (Chicago: University of Chicago Press, 2007).

15. Schwartzman, *Black Unemployment*.

16. William Julius Wilson, *The Truly Disadvantaged: The Inner City, the Underclass, and Public Policy* (Chicago: University of Chicago Press, 1987); and William Julius Wilson, *When Work Disappears: The World of the New Urban Poor* (New York: Knopf, 1996).

17. US Department of Housing and Urban Development, *The State of Cities* (Washington, DC: Government Printing Office, 1999).

18. Wilson, *When Work Disappears*.

19. US Department of Housing and Urban Development, *State of Cities*.

20. A more detailed account of the transportation and networking problems of poor black workers is provided in Wilson, *When Work Disappears*.

21. See Frank Levy, *The New Dollars and Dreams: American Incomes and Economic Change* (New York: Sage Foundation, 1998).

22. According to sociologists Bruce Western and Becky Pettit, the recorded employment gains of low-skilled black men during the economic boom of the 1990s were the artifact of the major expansion of mass black imprisonment during this period. And according to their analysis, if the numbers of incarcerated blacks were added to the official employment statistics, the gains would disappear. Bruce Western and Becky Pettit, "Incarceration and Racial Inequality in Men's Employment," *Industrial*

and Labor Relations Review 54 (2000), 3–16. However, this position has been challenged by University of Wisconsin sociologist Felix Elwert, whose formal quantitative model suggests the opposite conclusion: that incarceration has likely increased rather than decreased low-skilled black unemployment rates. Felix Elwert, "The Effects of Incarceration on Aggregate Unemployment Rates" (unpublished manuscript, University of Wisconsin, 2008).

23. In 2007, a single person with an annual income of $9,800 and a family of four with an annual income of $33,600 were classified as poor.

24. In Chapter 5, however, I will discuss and explain why some legislation during the George W. Bush administration that can be tied to Clinton's welfare reform policy actually benefited the working poor.

25. My discussion in this section on the concept of culture owes a great deal to the work of Michèle Lamont and Mario Luis Small. See their "How Culture Matters for the Understanding of Poverty: Enriching Our Understanding," in *The Color of Poverty: Why Racial and Ethnic Disparities Exist*, eds. David Harris and Ann Lin (New York: Sage Foundation, forthcoming).

26. For a review of the literature on school tracking, see Janese Free, "Race and School Tracking: From a Social Psychological Perspective" (paper, American Sociological Association, San Francisco, August 14, 2004).

27. Lawrence Bobo, James R. Kluegel, and Ryan A. Smith, "Laissez Faire Racism: The Crystallization of a Kinder, Gentler, Antiblack Ideology," in *Racial Attitudes in the 1990s*, eds. Steven A. Tuch and Jack K. Martin (Westport, CT: Praeger, 1997), 15–44.

28. Wilson, *When Work Disappears*.

29. Charles Tilly, *Durable Inequality* (Berkeley: University of California Press, 1998).

30. There is mixed evidence for the outcomes of "acting white" as it applies to education. One of the best-known studies of this concept was published by Signithia Fordham and John Ogbu in 1986. They studied African American students at a high school in Washington DC and concluded that the fear of acting white was one of the major factors undermining student achievement. Signithia Fordham and John Ogbu, "Black Students' School Success: Coping with the Burden of 'Acting White,'" *Urban Journal* 18 (1986), 176–206. In contrast, Prudence Carter's studies have not supported the idea that students who avoided "acting white" held lower educational aspirations. Prudence L. Carter, "'Black' Cultural Capital, Status Positioning, and Schooling Conflicts for Low-Income African American Youth," *Social Problems* 50 (2003), 136–55; and Prudence L. Carter, *Keepin' It Real: School Success Beyond Black and White* (New York: Oxford University Press, 2005). Roland Fryer presents yet another perspective. He found that a high grade point average (GPA) presents a social disadvantage for Hispanics and blacks in integrated schools and public schools, but he saw no such effect in schools that were segregated (80 percent or more black) or private. He also noticed a marked difference in this effect among black boys and black girls; black boys in public, integrated schools were particularly susceptible to social ostracism as their GPAs increased, and were penalized seven times more than black students (including both genders) overall. Roland G. Fryer,

"'Acting White': The Social Price Paid by the Best and Brightest Minority Students," *Education Next*, Winter 2006, 53–59.

31. Elijah Anderson, *Code of the Street: Decency, Violence, and the Moral Life of the Inner City* (New York: W. W. Norton, 1999).

32. Sudhir Alladi Venkatesh, *Off the Books: The Underground Economy of the Urban Poor* (Cambridge, MA: Harvard University Press, 2006).

33. Anderson, *Code of the Street*, 34.

34. Venkatesh, *Off the Books*, 381.

35. Ibid, 377.

36. Ibid., 385. For another excellent study of how activities in the underground economy can adversely affect inner-city residents, see Loïc Wacquant, "Inside the Zone: The Art of the Hustler in the Black American Ghetto," *Theory, Culture, and Society* 15 (1998), 1–36.

37. Orlando Patterson, "A Poverty of the Mind," *New York Times*, March 26, 2006.

38. Ibid.

39. Ibid. See also Orlando Patterson, "Taking Culture Seriously: A Framework and an Afro-American Illustration," in *Culture Matters: How Values Shape Human Progress*, eds. Lawrence E. Harrison and Samuel P. Huntington (New York: Basic Books, 2000), 202–18.

40. Neckerman, *Schools Betrayed*.

41. Ibid., 174.

42. Patterson, "Poverty of the Mind," 13.

43. Ibid.

CHAPTER 2.

1. William Julius Wilson, *When Work Disappears: The World of the New Urban Poor* (New York: Knopf, 1996).

2. Paul Jargowsky, "Ghetto Poverty among Blacks in the 1980s," *Journal of Policy Analysis and Management* 13 (1994), 288–310.

3. See the following chapters in *The "Underclass" Debate: Views from History*, ed. Michael B. Katz (Princeton, NJ: Princeton University Press, 1993): Michael B. Katz, "Reframing the 'Underclass' Debate," 440–78; David W. Bartelt, "Housing the 'Underclass,'" 118–57; Thomas J. Sugrue, "The Structure of Urban Poverty: The Reorganization of Space and Work in Three Periods of American History," 85–117; and Robin D. G. Kelley, "The Black Poor and the Politics of Opposition in a New South City," 293–333.

4. Katz, "Reframing the 'Underclass' Debate," 462. See also Bartelt "Housing the 'Underclass'"; Sugrue, "Structure of Urban Poverty"; and Martin Anderson, *The Federal Bulldozer: A Critical Analysis of Urban Renewal, 1949–1962* (Cambridge, MA: MIT Press, 1964).

5. Raymond Mohl, "Planned Destruction: The Interstates and Central City Housing," in *From Tenements to Taylor Homes: In Search of an Urban Housing Policy in*

Twentieth-Century America, eds. John F. Bauman, Roger Biles, and Kristin Szyl-
vian (University Park, PA: State University Press, 2000), 226–45; Adam Cohen
and Elizabeth Taylor, *American Pharaoh: Mayor Richard J. Daley—His Battle for
Chicago and Nation* (Boston: Little, Brown, 2000); Arnold R. Hirsch, *Making the
Second Ghetto: Race and Housing in Chicago, 1940–1960* (Cambridge: Cambridge
University Press, 1983).

6. Cohen and Taylor, *American Pharaoh*.

7. Charles E. Connerly, "From Racial Zoning to Community Empowerment: The
Interstate Highway System and the African American Community in Birmingham,
Alabama," *Journal of Planning Education and Research* 22 (1992), 99–114.

8. Connerly, "From Racial Zoning"; Ronald H. Bayor, "Roads to Racial Segregation:
Atlanta in the Twentieth Century," *Journal of Urban History* 15 (1988), 3–21.

9. Katz, "Reframing the 'Underclass' Debate"; Kenneth T. Jackson, *Crabgrass Frontier:
The Suburbanization of the United States* (New York: Oxford University Press, 1985);
and Ira Katznelson, *When Affirmative Action Was White: An Untold History of Racial
Inequality in Twentieth-Century America* (New York: W. W. Norton, 2005).

10. Robert J. Sampson and William Julius Wilson, "Toward a Theory of Race, Crime,
and Urban Inequality," in *Crime and Inequality*, eds. John Hagan and Ruth Peterson
(Stanford, CA: Stanford University Press, 1995), 37–54.

11. Rosalyn Baxandall and Elizabeth Ewen, *Picture Windows: How the Suburbs Happened* (New York: Basic Books, 2000).

12. Katz, "Reframing the 'Underclass' Debate," 461–62. On the history of suburbs in
America, see Jackson, *Crabgrass Frontier*. For a good discussion of the effects of
housing discrimination on the living conditions, education, and employment of
urban minorities, see John Yinger, *Closed Doors, Opportunities Lost: The Continuing Costs of Housing Discrimination* (New York: Sage Foundation, 1995).

13. Mark Condon, *Public Housing, Crime and the Urban Labor Market: A Study of Black
Youth in Chicago*, Working Paper Series, no. H-91-3 (Cambridge, MA: Malcolm Wie-
ner Center, John F. Kennedy School of Government, Harvard University, 1991).

14. Ibid., 3.

15. Ibid., 4.

16. Ibid., 4.

17. Sampson and Wilson, "Toward a Theory of Race." See also Bartelt, "Housing the
'Underclass'"; Kelley, "Black Poor and the Politics of Opposition"; Sugrue, "Structure
of Urban Poverty"; Arnold R. Hirsch, *Making the Second Ghetto*; and John F. Bauman, Norman P. Hummon, and Edward K. Muller, "Public Housing Isolation, and
the Urban Underclass," *Journal of Urban History* 17 (1991), 264–92.

18. Lincoln Quillian, "Migration Patterns and the Growth of High-Poverty Neighborhoods, 1970–1990," *American Journal of Sociology* 105 (1999), 1–37.

19. Ibid.

20. Ibid.

21. William Julius Wilson, *The Truly Disadvantaged: The Inner City, the Underclass, and*

Public Policy (Chicago: University of Chicago Press, 1987); Wilson, *When Work Disappears*; Quillian, *Migration Patterns*.

22. See Demetrios Caraley, "Washington Abandons the Cities," *Political Science Quarterly* 107 (Spring 1992), 1–30.

23. Bruce A. Wallin, *Budgeting for Basics: The Changing Landscape of City Finances*, Discussion paper prepared for the Brookings Institution Metropolitan Policy Program (Washington, DC: Brookings Institution, August 2005).

24. Caraley, "Washington Abandons the Cities."

25. US Department of Housing and Urban Development, *The State of Cities* (Washington, DC: Government Printing Office, 1999).

26. Caraley, "Washington Abandons the Cities."

27. Iris J. Lav and Andrew Brecher, *Passing Down the Deficit: Federal Policies Contribute to the Severity of the State Fiscal Crisis* (Washington, DC: Center on Budget and Policy Priorities, May 12, 2004).

28. Bruce Katz, "Beyond City Limits: The Emergence of a New Metropolitan Agenda" (unpublished manuscript, Brookings Institution, 1999).

29. Economists Linda Bilmes and Joseph E. Stiglitz estimate that the final cost for the Iraq war will be between $1 trillion and $2 trillion, depending on how much longer U.S. soldiers remain in Iraq. See Linda Bilmes and Joseph Stiglitz, "The Economic Costs of the Iraq War: An Appraisal Three Years after the Beginning of the Conflict" (paper, Allied Social Science Association, Boston, MA, January 6–8, 2006).

30. US Department of Labor, "Federal Minimum Wage Rates under the Fair Labor Standards Act" (2008), at www.dol.gov/esa/minwage/chart.pdf.

31. Radhika K. Fox and Sarah Treuhaft, *Shared Prosperity, Stronger Regions: An Agenda for Rebuilding America's Older Core Cities* (Oakland, CA: PolicyLink, 2006).

32. Bill Joy, "Why the Future Doesn't Need Us," *Wired*, April 2000, 238–62; and Fox and Treuhaft, *Shared Prosperity, Stronger Regions*.

33. Wilson, *When Work Disappears*.

34. Fox and Treuhaft, *Shared Prosperity, Stronger Regions*.

35. Ibid.

36. Fox and Treuhaft, *Shared Prosperity, Stronger Regions*; Wilson, *When Work Disappears*.

37. US Department of Housing and Urban Development, *State of Cities*.

38. Fox and Treuhaft, *Shared Prosperity, Stronger Regions*.

39. Ibid., 32.

40. Fox and Treuhaft, *Shared Prosperity, Stronger Regions*.

41. See, for example, Wilson, *When Work Disappears*; and Joleen Kirschenman and Kathryn Neckerman, "We'd Love to Hire Them, but . . . : The Meaning of Race for Employers," in *The Urban Underclass*, eds. Christopher Jencks and Paul E. Peterson (Washington, DC: Brookings Institution, 1991), 203–34; Kathryn M. Neckerman and Joleen Kirschenman, "Hiring Strategies, Racial Bias, and Inner-City Workers," *Social Problems* 38 (November 1991), 433–47; and Harry Holzer, *What Employers*

Want: Job Prospects for Less Educated Workers (New York: Sage Foundation, 1996).

42. Wilson, *Truly Disadvantaged*; Wilson, *When Work Disappears*; and Fox and Treuhaft, *Shared Prosperity, Stronger Regions*.

43. Fox and Treuhaft, *Shared Prosperity, Stronger Regions*.

44. Wilson, *Truly Disadvantaged*; and Wilson, *When Work Disappears*.

45. Richard Majors and Janet Billson, *Cool Pose* (Lexington, MA: Heath, 1992); Orlando Patterson, "Taking Culture Seriously: A Framework and Afro-American Illustration," in *Culture Matters: How Values Shape Human Progress*, eds. Lawrence E. Harrison and Samuel P. Huntington (New York: Basic Books, 2000), 202–18; Orlando Patterson, "A Poverty of the Mind," *New York Times*, March 26, 2006.

46. James R. Kluegel and Eliot R. Smith, *Beliefs about Inequality: Americans' Views of What Is and What Ought to Be* (New York: de Gruyter, 1986). See also James R. Kluegel and Eliot R. Smith, "Affirmative Action Attitudes, Effects of Self-Interest, Racial Affect, and Stratification Beliefs on Whites' Views," *Social Forces* 61 (1983), 797–824.

47. Lawrence Bobo and Ryan A. Smith, "Antipoverty Politics, Affirmative Action, and Racial Attitudes," in *Confronting Poverty: Prescriptions for Change*, eds. Sheldon H. Danziger, Gary D. Sandefur, and Daniel H. Weinberg (Cambridge, MA: Harvard University Press, 1994), 365–95.

48. *Blacks See Growing Values Gap between Poor and Middle Class: Optimism about Black Progress Declines* (Washington, DC: Pew Research Center, November 13, 2007), 33.

49. Ibid.

50. Commission of the European Communities, *The Perception of Poverty in Europe* (Brussels: European Commission, 1990).

51. Commission of the European Communities, *Poverty and Exclusion* (Brussels: European Commission, 2007).

52. For a summary of some of the important studies on neighborhood effects, see Mario L. Small and Kathryn K. Newman, "Urban Poverty after The Truly Disadvantaged: The Rediscovery of the Family, the Neighborhood, and Culture," *Annual Review of Sociology* 27 (2001), 23–45.

53. John Quigley and Steven Raphael, "Neighborhoods, Economic Self-Sufficiency, and the MTO," *Brookings-Wharton Papers on Urban Affairs*, 2008, 3.

54. See, for example, William N. Evans, Wallace E. Oates, and Robert M. Schwab, "Measuring Peer Group Effects: A Study of Teenage Behavior," *Journal of Political Economy* 100 (1992), 966–91; and Robert Plotnick and Saul Hoffman, "Using Sister Pairs to Estimate How Neighborhoods Affect Young Adult Outcomes," Working Papers in Public Policy Analysis and Management, No. 93-8 (Seattle, WA: Graduate School of Public Affairs, University of Washington, 1993). For a good discussion of the issue of self-selection bias, see Paul Jargowsky, *Poverty and Place: Ghettos, Barrios, and the American City* (New York: Sage Foundation, 1997).

55. James E. Rosenbaum and Susan Popkin, "Employment and Earnings of Low-Income Blacks Who Move to Middle-Class Suburbs," in *The Urban Underclass*, eds. Christopher Jencks and Paul E. Peterson (Washington, DC: Brookings Institution,

1991), 342–56; James Rosenbaum, Stefanie DeLuca, and Tammy Tuck, *Moving and Changing: How Places Change People Who Move into Them*, Institute for Policy Research Working Paper, WP-02-09 (Evanston, IL: IPR, 2002); J. E. Kaufman and J. Rosenbaum, *The Education and Employment of Low-Income Black Youth in White Suburbs*, Institute for Policy Research Working Paper, WP-91-20 (Evanston, IL: IPR, 1991), published in *Educational Evaluation & Policy Analysis* 14 (1992), 229–40; James E. Rosenbaum, Susan J. Popkin, Julie E. Kaufman, and Jennifer Rusin, *Social Integration of Low-Income Black Adults in White Middle-Class Suburbs*, Institute for Policy Research Working Paper, WP-91-06 (Evanston, IL: IPR, 1991), published in *Social Problems* 38 (1991), 448–61; and J. Rosenbaum and S. Popkin, *Economic and Social Impacts of Housing Integration: A Report to the Charles Stewart Mott Foundation* (Evanston, IL: IPR, Northwestern University, 1990).

56. Susan Clampet-Lundquist and Douglas S. Massey, "Neighborhood Effects on Economic Self-Sufficiency: A Reconstruction of the Moving to Opportunity Experiment," *American Journal of Sociology* 114 (2008), 109–45.

57. Micere Keels, Greg J. Duncan, Stefanie DeLuca, Ruby Mendenhall, and James Rosenbaum, "Fifteen Years Later: Can Residential Mobility Programs Provide a Long Term Escape from Neighborhood Segregation, Crime, and Poverty?" *Demography* 42 (2006), 51–73.

58. Jeffrey R. Kling, Jeffrey B. Lieberman, Lawrence F. Katz, and Lisa Sanbonatsu, *Moving to Opportunities and Tranquility: Neighborhood Effects on Adult Economic Self-Sufficiency and Health from a Randomized Housing Voucher Experiment*, Princeton IRS Working Paper, No. 481 (Princeton, NJ: Princeton University, April 2004, revised October 2004), 31.

59. Robert J. Sampson, "Moving to Inequality: Neighborhood Effects and Experiments Meet Social Structure," *American Journal of Sociology* 114 (July 2008), 191–233.

60. Sampson, "Moving to Inequality"; Clampet-Lundquist and Massey, "Neighborhood Effects."

61. Stefanie DeLuca, "All over the Map: Explaining Educational Outcomes of the Moving to Opportunity Program," *Education Next*, Fall 2007, 25.

62. Quigley and Raphael, "Neighborhoods, Economic Self-Sufficiency."

63. Patrick Sharkey, "The Intergenerational Transmission of Context," *American Journal of Sociology* 113 (January 2008), 931–69.

64. Ibid.

65. Ibid., 963.

66. Robert J. Sampson, Patrick Sharkey, and Stephen W. Raudenbush, "Durable Effects of Concentrated Disadvantage on Verbal Ability among African-American Children," *Proceedings of the National Academy of Sciences of the United States of America* 105 (2008), 845–52.

67. Ibid., 846. Sampson and his colleagues created a composite measure of verbal ability based on results from two widely used tests given to their subjects: the Wide Range Achievement Test reading examination and the Wechsler Intelligence Scale for Children vocabulary test.

68. Ibid., 852.
69. Ibid., 845.
70. Ibid., 852.
71. Ibid., 852.
72. Ibid.
73. Sharkey, "Intergenerational Transmission of Context."
74. Erik Olin Wright, private communication, May 7, 2008.
75. Ibid. As Wright points out, this argument on enduring dispositions is consistent with Pierre Bourdieu's notion of "habitus." See Pierre Bourdieu, *In Other Words: Essays towards a Reflexive Sociology* (Stanford, CA: Stanford University Press, 1990). Also see Aurora P. Jackson, "The Effects of Family and Neighborhood Characteristics on the Behavioral and Cognitive Development of Poor Black Children: A Longitudinal Study," *American Journal of Community Psychology* 32 (2003), 175–86.
76. Jargowsky, *Poverty and Place*, 186.
77. Paul Jargowsky, *Stunning Progress, Hidden Problems: The Dramatic Decline of Concentrated Poverty in the 1990s* (Washington, DC: Brookings Institution, 2003).
78. Ibid., 9.
79. Ibid., 9.
80. Ibid., 4.
81. Ibid.

CHAPTER 3.

1. Elliot Liebow. *Tally's Corner: A Study of Street Corner Men* (Boston: Little Brown, 1967).
2. Ibid., 50–51.
3. Ibid., 51.
4. Part of what follows in this chapter is based on field research that my colleagues, graduate students, and I conducted in Chicago's inner-city neighborhoods from the mid-1980s to the mid-1990s. One of these research projects was the Urban Poverty and Family Life Study (UPFLS), conducted in 1987 and 1988, which included a random sample of nearly 2,500 poor and nonpoor African American, Latino, and white residents in Chicago's poor, inner-city neighborhoods. As part of this broad project, the UPFLS included data from three sources: (1) the Social Opportunity Survey, a subsample of 175 UPFLS participants who answered open-ended questions concerning their perceptions about their opportunities and life chances; (2) a 1988 survey of 179 employers—in most cases the information came from the highest-ranking official in the firm—selected to reflect the distribution of employment possibilities across industry and firm size in the Chicago metropolitan area; and (3) comprehensive ethnographic research—that is, participant-observation research and life history interviews—conducted during the period 1986 to 1988 by ten research assistants in a representative sample of inner-city neighborhoods. Other projects included a 1993 survey of a representative sample of 500 respondents from

two high-joblessness neighborhoods on Chicago's South Side and six focus group discussions involving the residents and former residents of these neighborhoods.

5. William Julius Wilson, *When Work Disappears: The World of the New Urban Poor* (New York: Knopf, 1996).

6. Ibid.

7. Allison K. Rodean and Christopher H. Wheeler, "Neighborhoods That Don't Work," *Regional Economist* (April 2008), at www.stls.frb.org/publications/re/2008/b/pages/neighborhoods.html.

8. Floyd Norris, "Many More Are Jobless Than Are Unemployed," *New York Times* (April 12, 2008), at www.nytimes.com/2008/04/12/business/12charts.html?ex=1365739200&en=90c9b2f19824f964&ei=5124&partner=permalink&exprod=permalink.

9. Ibid.

10. The figures in this paragraph were calculated from data provided by economist David Ellwood of Harvard University, based on data from the US Department of Labor.

11. Andrew Sum, Ishwar Khatiwada, Joseph McLaughlin, and Paulo Tobar, "The Educational Attainment of the Nation's Young Black Men and Their Recent Labor Market Experiences: What Can Be Done to Improve Their Future Labor Market and Educational Prospects?" (paper prepared for Jobs for America's Graduates, Alexandria, VA, February 2007).

12. Ibid., 2–3.

13. Ibid.

14. Lawrence Katz, *Wage Subsidies for the Disadvantaged*, Working Paper 5679 (Cambridge, MA: National Bureau of Economic Research, 1996); and David Schwartzman, *Black Unemployment: Part of Unskilled Unemployment* (Westport, CT: Greenwood Press, 1997).

15. John Schmitt and Ben Zipperer, *The Decline in African-American Representation in Unions and Manufacturing, 1979–2007* (Washington, DC: Center for Economic and Policy Research, February 2008).

16. John Schmitt and Ben Zipperer, *The Decline in African-American Representation in Unions and Manufacturing, 1979–2006* (Washington, DC: Center for Economic and Policy Research Report, March 2007).

17. Ibid.

18. Jean Anyon. *Ghetto Schooling: A Political Economy of Urban Educational Reform* (New York: Teachers College Press, 1997).

19. Bruce Western, *Punishment and Inequality in America* (New York: Sage Foundation, 2006).

20. Ibid., 79.

21. Ibid., 31. These figures on incarceration of black males were originally published in Becky Pettit and Bruce Western, "Mass Imprisonment and the Life Course: Race and Class Inequality in US Incarceration," *American Sociological Review* 69 (2004), 477–98.

22. Western, *Punishment and Inequality*, 79.

23. Ibid.

24. Harry J. Holzer, Paul Offner, and Elaine Sorensen, "What Explains the Continuing Decline in Labor Force Activity among Young Black Men?" (paper, Color Lines Conference, Harvard University, August 30, 2003).

25. Wilson, *When Work Disappears*. See also two other studies based on this research by members of our research team: Kathryn Neckerman and Joleen Kirschenman, "Hiring Strategies, Racial Bias, and Inner-City Workers," *Social Problems* 38 (November 1991), 433–47; and Joleen Kirschenman and Kathryn Neckerman, "We'd Love to Hire Them, but . . . : The Meaning of Race for Employers," in *The Urban Underclass*, eds. Christopher Jencks and Paul E. Peterson (Washington, DC: Brookings Institution, 1991), 203–34. Another relevant study is Harry Holzer, *What Employers Want: Job Prospects for Less-Educated Workers* (New York: Sage Foundation, 1995); and see also Philip Moss and Chris Tilly, *Stories Employers Tell: Race, Skill, and Hiring in America* (New York: Sage Foundation, 2001).

26. Wilson, *When Work Disappears*.

27. Sandra Susan Smith, *Lone Pursuit: Distrust and Defensive Individualism among the Black Poor* (New York: Sage Foundation, 2007).

28. Devah Pager, "The Mark of a Criminal Record," *American Journal of Sociology* 108 (2003), 937–75.

29. Erik Olin Wright, private communication, May 7, 2008. I am indebted to Wright for the insights expressed in this paragraph.

30. Holzer, Offner, and Sorensen, "What Explains the Continuing Decline?"

31. Jamie Peck and Nik Theodore, "Contingent Chicago: Restructuring the Spaces of Temporary Labor," *International Journal of Urban Research* 25 (2001), 492.

32. In addition to exacerbating the problem of joblessness, incarceration impairs the chances of successful participation in society in other ways. As Christopher Wildeman and Christopher Muller point out, "incarceration poses formidable legal barriers to political participation, the retention of parental rights, and the receipt of welfare, public housing, and financial aid (Travis 2002). In all but two states, incarcerated individuals are not allowed to vote, and ex-felons are not allowed to vote in many states. The 1997 Adoption and Safe Families Act speeds the termination of parental rights for children who have been in foster care for 15 of the last 22 months—a duration far shorter than the median prison sentence. An often-overlooked provision of welfare reform permanently prohibits individuals with drug-related felony convictions from receiving federal assistance and food stamps. Statutes enacted in the 1990s give public housing agencies the authority to deny housing to individuals with a wide array of criminal convictions. And the Higher Education Act of 1998 renders any individual convicted of a drug-related offense ineligible for student loans. Together, these legal barriers present formidable challenges to individuals seeking to return safely from prison—particularly given their diminished pre-incarceration resources." Christopher Wildeman and Christopher Muller, "Incarceration: Adulthood," in *Encyclopedia of the Life Course and Human Development*, ed. Deborah

Carr (Farmington Hills, MI: Gale Research, forthcoming). See also Jeremy Travis, "Invisible Punishment: An Instrument of Social Exclusion," in *Invisible Punishment: The Collateral Consequences of Mass Imprisonment*, eds. Marc Mauer and Meda Chesney-Lind (New York: New Press, 2002).

33. Wilson, *When Work Disappears*.

34. See, for example, the collection of research papers in Ronald B. Mincy, ed., *Black Males Left Behind* (Washington, DC: Urban Institute Press, 2006).

35. Orlando Patterson, "A Poverty of the Mind," *New York Times*, March 26, 2006.

36. Roger Waldinger, *Still the Promised City? African–Americans and New Immigrants in Postindustrial New York* (Cambridge MA: Harvard University Press, 1996).

37. Patterson, "Poverty of the Mind."

38. Ibid.

39. See Richard Majors and Janet Billson, *Cool Pose* (Lexington, MA: Heath, 1992); and Elijah Anderson, *Streetwise: Race, Class and Change in an Urban Community* (Chicago: University of Chicago Press, 1990).

40. Patterson, "Poverty of the Mind." Elijah Anderson supports this view on the basis of research in inner-city neighborhoods in Philadelphia. He argues that many young black males fail to take advantage of employment opportunities in the formal labor market when they become available because "the draw of the street [is] too powerful." Elijah Anderson, *Code of the Street: Decency, Violence, and the Moral Life of the Inner City* (New York: W. W. Norton, 1999; paperback 2000).

41. Orlando Patterson, "Taking Culture Seriously: A Framework and Afro-American Illustration," in *Culture Matters: How Values Shape Human Progress*, eds. Lawrence E. Harrison and Samuel P. Huntington (New York: Basic Books, 2000), 204.

42. Lee Rainwater, "Crucible of Identity: The Negro Lower-Class Family," *Daedalus* 95 (Winter 1966), 176–216.

43. Anderson, *Streetwise*; Majors and Billson, *Cool Pose*; and Carl Nightingale, *On the Edge: A History of Poor Black Children and Their American Dream* (New York: Basic Books, 1993).

44. Patterson, "Taking Culture Seriously."

45. Lawrence M. Mead, *The New Politics of Poverty: The Nonworking Poor in America* (New York: Basic Books, 1992).

46. Ibid., 149.

47. Mead makes reference to "comments by black scholars" to support this contention, including Orlando Patterson, "The Moral Crisis of the Black American," *Public Interest* no. 32 (Summer 1973), 43–69; Anne Wortham, *The Other Side of Racism: A Philosophical Study of Black Race Consciousness* (Columbus: Ohio State University Press, 1981); and Glenn Loury, "The Moral Quandary of the Black Community," *Public Interest* no. 79 (Spring 1985), 9–22. However, none of these writers provides any empirical evidence that would support Mead's claim. Mead is not citing their field research, but their thoughtful essays.

48. Katherine S. Newman, *No Shame in My Game: The Working Poor in the Inner City* (New York: Knopf and Sage Foundation, 1999).

49. Alford Young Jr., *The Minds of Marginalized Black Men: Making Sense of Mobility, Opportunity, and Future Life Chances* (Princeton, NJ: Princeton University Press, 2004).

50. See also Young, *Minds of Marginalized Black Men.*

51. Wilson, *When Work Disappears.* See also Roberta Iversen and Naomi Farber, "Transmission of Family Values, Work and Welfare among Poor Urban Black Women," *Work and Occupations* 23 (1996), 437–60; and Rachel Jones and Ye Lou, "The Culture of Poverty and African-American Culture: Empirical Assessment," *Sociological Perspectives* 42 (1999), 439–58.

52. Jennifer L. Hochschild, *Facing Up to the American Dream: Race, Class, and the Soul of the Nation* (Princeton, NJ: Princeton University Press, 1995).

53. Smith, *Lone Pursuit,* 167.

54. Hochschild, *Facing Up to the American Dream,* 218.

55. Patterson, "Poverty of the Mind"; Waldinger, *Still the Promised City?*

56. Mead, *New Politics of Poverty.*

57. Waldinger, *Still the Promised City?*

58. See Harry J. Holzer, "Black Youth Nonemployment: Duration and Job Search," in *Black Youth Employment Crisis,* eds. Richard Freeman and Harry Holzer (Chicago: University of Chicago Press, 1986), 23–73.

59. Smith, *Lone Pursuit,* 12.

60. Ibid.

61. Mary Waters, *Black Identities: West Indian Immigrant Dreams and American Realities* (Cambridge, MA: Harvard University Press, 1999).

62. Stephen Petterson, "Are Young Black Men Really Less Willing to Work?" *American Sociological Review* 62 (August 1997), 605–13.

63. Ibid., 606.

64. Ibid., 606.

65. See, for example, Holzer, "Black Youth Nonemployment"; and Harry Holzer, "Reservation Wages and Their Labor Market Effects for Black and White Male Youth," *Journal of Human Resources* 21 (1986), 157–77.

66. Petterson, "Are Young Black Men Really Less Willing?" 207.

67. See, Holzer, "Black Youth Nonemployment"; Holzer, "Reservation Wages"; Stephen R. G. Jones, "The Relationship between Unemployment Spells and Reservation Wages as a Test of Search Theory," *Quarterly Journal of Economics* 103 (1988), 741–65; and Peter Jensen and Niels C. Westergard-Nielson, "A Search Model Applied to the Transition from Education to Work," *Review of Economic Studies* 54 (1987), 461–72.

68. Petterson, "Are Young Black Men Really Less Willing?" 609.

69. Ibid.

70. Ibid., 612.

71. Stephen Petterson, "Black-White Differences in Joblessness among Young Men: The Limits of Cultural Explanations" (PhD dissertation, University of Wisconsin, 1994).

72. Ibid., 612.

73. The willingness of low-skilled workers with few options to accept menial employment is perhaps most clearly revealed in Katherine Newman and Chauncy Lennon's study of fast-food restaurants in New York City, in which they found that there were fourteen applicants for every job vacancy. Katherine S. Newman and Chauncy Lennon, *Finding Work in the Inner City: How Hard Is It Now? How Hard Will It Be for AFDC Recipients?* Working Paper 76 (New York: Sage Foundation, 1995).

74. Smith, *Lone Pursuit.*

75. Ibid.

76. Sophie Pedder, "Social Isolation and the Labor Market: Black Americans in Chicago" (paper, Chicago Urban Poverty and Family Life Conference, Chicago, IL, October 10–12, 1991).

77. Ibid., 37.

78. Ibid., 23.

79. Ibid.

CHAPTER 4.

1. Adam Clymer, "Daniel Patrick Moynihan Is Dead; Senator from Academia Was 76," *New York Times*, March 27, 2003.

2. Daniel P. Moynihan, *The Negro Family: The Case for National Action* (Washington, DC: Office of Planning and Research, US Department of Labor, 1965), 30.

3. Lee Rainwater and William L. Yancey, *The Moynihan Report and the Politics of Controversy* (Cambridge, MA: MIT Press, 1967), 144.

4. Ibid., 154.

5. See, for example, Robert H. Hill, *The Strength of Black Families* (New York: Emerson Hall, 1972); Abdul Hakim Ibn Alkalimat (Gerald McWorter), "The Ideology of Black Social Science," *Black Scholar* 1 (December 1969), 28–35; Nathan Hare, "The Challenge of a Black Scholar," *Black Scholar* 1 (December 1969), 58–63; Robert Staples, "The Myth of the Black Matriarchy," *Black Scholar* 2 (February 1970), 9–16; Robert Staples, *The Black Family: Essays and Studies* (Belmont, CA: Wadsworth, 1971); and Joyce Ladner, ed., *The Death of White Sociology* (New York: Random House, 1973).

6. As the sociologist Robert K. Merton points out, "when a once powerless collectivity acquires a socially validated sense of growing power, its members experience an intensified need for self-affirmation. Under such conditions, collective self-glorification, found in some measure among all groups, becomes a predictable and intensified counter response to long-standing belittlement from without." Robert K. Merton, "Insiders and Outsiders: A Chapter in the Sociology of Knowledge," *American Journal of Sociology* 78 (July 1972), 18–19.

7. See, for example, Hare, "Challenge of a Black Scholar"; and Alkalimat, "Ideology of Black Social Science." This rejection even included the thoughtful argument, so clearly articulated by Kenneth Clark and Lee Rainwater in the latter 1960s, that

the logical outcome of racial isolation and class subordination is that individuals are forced to adapt to the realities of the ghetto community and are therefore seriously impaired in their ability to function in any other community. See Kenneth B. Clark, *Dark Ghetto: Dilemmas of Social Power* (New York: Harper & Row, 1965); and Lee Rainwater, "Crucible of Identity: The Negro Lower-Class Family," *Daedalus* 95 (Winter 1966), 176–216.

8. US Department of Health and Human Services, *Nonmarital Childbearing in the United States, 1940–1999*, National Vital Statistics Reports, Vol. 48, No. 16 (Washington, DC: Government Printing Office, 2000); Brady E. Hamilton, Joyce A. Martin, and Stephanie J. Ventura, "Births: Preliminary Data for 2005," NCHS Health E-Stats, at www.cdc.gov/nchs/products/pubs/pubd/hestats/prelimbirths05/prelim births05.htm (accessed September 20, 2007).

9. US Bureau of the Census, *Household and Family Characteristics*, Current Population Survey, Series P20-495 (Washington, DC: Government Printing Office, March 1996), table 1; and US Bureau of the Census, Population Division, "Current Population Survey, 2006 Annual Social and Economic Supplement," table F1, at www .census.gov/population/socdemo/hh-fam/cps2006/tabF1-all.xls (accessed September 20, 2007).

10. Greg J. Duncan, *Years of Poverty, Years of Plenty* (Ann Arbor: Institute for Social Research, University of Michigan, 1984).

11. US Bureau of the Census, "American Community Survey" (2006), table B02001, at http://factfinder.census.gov/servlet/DatasetMainPageServlet?_program=ACS& _submenuId=datasets_2&_lang=en&_ts=.

12. Kathryn Edin, "The Myths of Dependence and Self-Sufficiency: Women, Welfare, and Low-Wage Work," *Focus* 17 (1995), 203–30.

13. For married couples, this information comes from US Bureau of the Census, "American Community Survey" (2006), table B19126 ("Median income") and table B17006 ("Poverty status of children"), at http://factfinder.census.gov/servlet/DatasetMain PageServlet?_program=ACS&_submenuId=datasets_2&_lang=en&_ts=; for single-mother families, from an analysis of microdata in US Bureau of the Census, "American Community Survey" (2006).

14. For a review of this research, see Adam Thomas and Isabel Sawhill, "For Richer or Poorer: Marriage as an Antipoverty Strategy," *Journal of Policy Analysis and Management* 15 (2002), 587–99.

15. David Ellwood and Mary Jo Bane, *The Impact of AFDC on Family Structure and Living Arrangements*, Research in Labor Economics, Vol. 7 (Greenwich, CT: JAI Press, 1985); June E. O'Neill, Douglas Wolf, Laurie Bassi, and Michael Hannan, *An Analysis of Time on Welfare*, US Department of Health and Human Services Report, Contract No. HHS-100-83-0048 (Washington, DC: Urban Institute, 1984).

16. Mollie A. Martin, "Family Structure and Income Inequality in Families with Children," *Demography* 43 (2006), 421–46; Paul Amato, "The Impact of Family Formation Change on Cognitive, Social and Emotional Well-Being of the Next Generation," *Future of Children* 15 (2005), 75–96; Sara McLanahan, "Diverging Destinies: How

Children Are Faring under the Second Demographic Transition," *Demography* 41 (2004), 607–27; Sara McLanahan and Gary Sandefur, *Growing Up with a Single Parent: What Helps, What Hurts* (Cambridge MA: Harvard University Press, 1994); Sara McLanahan and Irwin Garfinkel, "Single Mothers, the Underclass, and Social Policy," *Annals of the American Academy of Political and Social Science* 501 (January 1989), 130–52; Sara McLanahan and Larry Bumpass, "Intergenerational Consequences of Family Disruption," *American Journal of Sociology* 94 (1988), 130–52; and Sheila Fitzgerald Krein and Andrea H. Beller, "Educational Attainment of Children from Single-Parent Families: Differences by Exposure, Gender and Race," *Demography* 25 (May 1988), 221–24.

17. Deborah Roempke Graefe and Daniel T. Lichter, "Marriage among Unwed Mothers: Whites, Blacks and Hispanics Compared," *Perspectives on Sexual and Reproductive Health* 34 (2002), 286–92.

18. Marcia Carlson, Sara McLanahan, and Paula England, "Union Formation in Fragile Families," *Demography* 41 (2004), 237–61.

19. Martha Van Haitsma, "A Contextual Definition of the Underclass," *Focus* 12 (Spring-Summer 1989), 27–31.

20. Lena Lundgren-Gaveras, "Informal Network Support, Public Welfare Support and the Labor Force Activity of Urban Low-Income Single Mothers" (paper, Chicago Urban Poverty and Family Life Conference, Chicago, IL, October 10–12, 1991).

21. Ibid.

22. The proportion of nonmarital births among whites and Latinos reached 24.5 and 46.4 percent, respectively, in 2005. Hamilton, Martin, and Ventura, "Births."

23. Thomas and Sawhill, "For Richer or Poorer."

24. See, for example, Greg J. Duncan's testimony before the Subcommittee on Human Resources of the Committee on Ways and Means Hearing on Early Childbearing, Washington, DC, July 29, 1994; and Saul D. Hoffman, Gregory J. Duncan, and Ronald B. Mincy, "Marriage and Welfare Use among Young Women: Do Labor Market, Welfare and Neighborhood Factors Account for Declining Rates of Marriage among Black and White Women?" (paper, American Economics Association, New Orleans, December 1991).

25. Duncan, testimony, July 29, 1994.

26. For a thorough discussion of shifting marriage norms over time, see Andrew Cherlin, "The Deinstitutionalization of American Marriage," *Journal of Marriage and Family* 66 (2004), 848–61.

27. These figures are based on an analysis of microdata from US Bureau of the Census, "American Community Survey" (2006), at http://factfinder.census.gov/ servlet/DatasetMainPageServlet?_program=ACS&_submenuId=datasets_2& _lang=en&_ts=.

28. Christopher Jencks, "Is the American Underclass Growing?" in *The Urban Underclass*, eds. Christopher Jencks and Paul Peterson (Washington, DC: Brookings Institution, 1991), 28–102.

29. For a good review of these studies, see David Ellwood and Christopher Jencks, "The

Uneven Spread of Single Parent Families in the United States. What Do We Know? Where Do We Look for Answers?" in *Social Inequality*, ed. Kathryn Neckerman (New York: Sage Foundation, 2004), 3–78.

30. Mark Testa and Marilyn Krogh, "The Effects of Employment on Marriage among Males in Inner-City Chicago," in *The Decline in Marriage among African Americans: Causes, Consequences and Policy Implications*, eds. M. Belinda Tucker and Claudia Mitchell-Kernan (New York: Sage Foundation, 1995), 59–95.

31. William Ryan, *Blaming the Victim* (New York: Pantheon, 1971).

32. Oscar Lewis, "The Culture of Poverty," in *On Understanding Poverty: Perspectives from the Social Sciences*, ed. Daniel Patrick Moynihan (New York: Basic Books, 1968), 188. See also Oscar Lewis, *Five Families: Mexican Case Studies in the Culture of Poverty* (New York: Basic Books, 1959); Oscar Lewis, *The Children of Sanchez* (New York: Random House, 1961); and Oscar Lewis, *La Vida: A Puerto Rican Family in the Culture of Poverty—San Juan and New York* (New York: Random House, 1966).

33. See, for example, Edward Banfield, *The Unheavenly City*, 2nd ed. (Boston: Little Brown, 1970).

34. Moynihan, *Negro Family*, 93.

35. Alice O'Connor, *Poverty and Knowledge: Social Science, Social Policy, and the Poor in Twentieth-Century U.S. History* (Princeton, NJ: Princeton University Press, 2001).

36. Orlando Patterson, "Culture and Continuity: Causal Structures in Socio-Cultural Persistence," in *Matters of Culture: Cultural Sociology in Practice*, eds. Roger Friedland and John Mohr (New York: Cambridge University Press, 2004), 71–109.

37. Ibid., 71.

38. Herbert G. Gutman, *The Black Family in Slavery and Freedom, 1750–1925* (New York: Pantheon, 1976).

39. Ibid., 80.

40. Samuel H. Preston, Suet Lim, and S. Philip Morgan, "African-American Marriage in 1910: Beneath the Surface of Census Data," *Demography* 29 (February 1992), 1–15; S. Philip Morgan, Antonio McDaniel, Andrew T. Miller, and Samuel H. Preston, "Racial Differences in Household and Family Structure at the Turn of the Century," *American Journal of Sociology* 98 (January 1993), 798–828.

41. Preston, Lim, and Morgan, "African-American Marriage," 1.

42. Ibid.

43. Morgan et al., "Racial Differences," 822.

44. See, for example, St. Clair Drake, *The Redemption of Africa and Black Religion* (Chicago: Third World Press, 1970); and George E. Simpson, *Black Religions in the New World* (New York: Columbia University Press, 1978).

45. Morgan et al., "Racial Differences," 823.

46. For my critical discussion of the cultural continuity thesis in this chapter, I am indebted to Tommie Shelby, private communication, July 10, 2008.

47. Morgan et al., "Racial Differences," 824.

48. Orlando Patterson, *Rituals of Blood: Consequences of Slavery in Two American Centuries* (New York: Basic Books, 1998).

49. Ellwood and Jencks, "Uneven Spread," 52.

50. Michèle Lamont and Mario Luis Small, "How Culture Matters for the Understanding of Poverty: Thickening Our Understanding," in *The Color of Poverty: Why Racial and Ethnic Disparities Exist*, eds. David Harris and Ann Lin (New York: Sage Foundation, forthcoming).

51. Ibid.

52. Ibid.

53. Mark Testa, "Male Joblessness, Nonmarital Parenthood and Marriage" (paper, Chicago Urban and Family Life Conference, Chicago, October 10–12, 1991), 16.

54. Ibid.

55. Our survey—the Urban Poverty and Family Life Study (UPFLS), conducted in 1987 and 1988—included a random sample of nearly 2,500 poor and nonpoor African American, Latino, and white residents in Chicago's poor, inner-city neighborhoods and is discussed in Chapter 3. Inner-city neighborhoods were defined in this study as those with poverty rates of at least 20 percent.

56. Testa, "Male Joblessness"; Testa and Krogh, "Effects of Unemployment"; and Martha Van Haitsma, "A Contextual Definition of the Underclass," *Focus* 12 (Spring–Summer 1991), 27–31.

57. Richard P. Taub, "Differing Conceptions of Honor and Orientations among Low-Income African-Americans and Mexican-Americans" (paper, Chicago Urban Poverty and Family Life Conference, Chicago, IL, October 10–12, 1991), 6.

58. Ibid.

59. Julie A. Phillips and Megan M. Sweeney, "Premarital Cohabitation and Marital Disruption among White, Black, and Mexican American Women," *Journal of Marriage and Family* 67 (May 2005), 296–314. See also R. S. Oropesa, Daniel T. Lichter, and Robert N. Anderson, "Marriage Markets and the Paradox of Mexican American Nuptiality," *Journal of Marriage and the Family* 56 (1994), 889–907.

60. This general distrust has also been documented by Kathryn Edin and by Christina Gibson-Davis and her colleagues. They note that women are wary of getting married in part because they are afraid that their partners will try to take more control of the household and start ordering them around. See K. Edin, "What Do Low-Income Single Mothers Say about Marriage?" *Social Problems* 47 (2000), 112–33; and Christina Gibson-Davis, Kathryn Edin, and Sara McLanahan, "High Hopes but Even Higher Expectations: The Retreat from Marriage among Low-Income Couples," *Journal of Marriage and Family* 67 (2005), 1301–12. The concerns over infidelity have also been documented in Paula K. England, Kathryn Edin, and K. Linnenberg, "Love and Distrust among Unmarried Parents" (paper, National Poverty Center Conference on Marriage and Family Formation among Low-Income Couples, Washington, DC, September 4–5, 2003).

61. Taub, "Differing Conceptions," 9.

62. Robert Laseter, "Young Inner-City African American Men: Work and Family Life" (PhD dissertation, University of Chicago, 1994), 195.

63. Although marriage behavior varies by racial/ethnic and socioeconomic groups, support for the institution of marriage is relatively evenly widespread. Indeed, 70 percent of welfare recipients say they expect to marry. Low-income and minority women voice doubts about marriage to their current partners but nonetheless show a high level of support for the institution of marriage overall. See D. T. Lichter, C. D. Batson, and J. D. Brown, "Welfare Reform and Marriage Promotion: The Marital Expectations and Desires of Single and Cohabiting Mothers," *Social Service Review* 78 (2004), 2–24; R. Kelly Raley, "Recent Trends and Differentials in Marriage and Cohabitation: The United States," in *The Ties That Bind: Perspectives on Marriage and Cohabitation*, ed. Linda J. Waite (New York: Aldine de Gruyter, 2000), 19–39; Jane G. Mauldon, Rebecca A. London, David J. Fein, Rhiannon Patterson, and Steven Bliss, *What Do They Think? Welfare Recipients' Attitudes toward Marriage and Childbearing* (Cambridge, MA: Abt Associates, 2002).

64. Frank F. Furstenberg Jr., "Fathering in the Inner City: Paternal Participation and Public Policy" (unpublished manuscript, University of Pennsylvania, 1994).

65. Laseter, "Young Inner-City African American Men," 40.

66. Furstenberg, "Fathering in the Inner City," 29.

67. Kathryn Edin and Maria Kefalas, *Promises I Can Keep: Why Poor Women Put Motherhood before Marriage* (Berkeley: University of California Press, 2005).

68. Diana Pearce, "Feminization of Poverty: Work and Welfare," *Urban and Social Change Review* 11 (1978), 146–60.

69. Douglas J. Besharov, *Measuring Poverty after Katrina* (Washington, DC: American Enterprise Institute, 2006).

70. Eugene M. Lewit, "Children in Poverty," *Future of Children* 3 (Spring 1993), 179.

71. Ibid., 180.

72. Greg J. Duncan. "The Economic Environment of Childhood," in *Children in Poverty*, ed. Althea C. Huston (Cambridge, MA: Cambridge University Press, 1991), 23–50.

73. See, for example, Lewit, "Children in Poverty."

74. I would like to thank Mario Small for this insight.

75. Daniel Breslau, "Reciprocity and Gender in Low-Income Households" (paper, Chicago Urban Poverty and Family Life Conference, Chicago, IL, October 10–12, 1991).

76. See Ellwood and Jencks, "Uneven Spread."

CHAPTER 5.

1. William Julius Wilson, *The Truly Disadvantaged: The Inner City, the Underclass, and Public Policy* (Chicago: University of Chicago Press, 1987); and William Julius Wilson, *When Work Disappears: The World of the New Urban Poor* (New York: Knopf, 1996).

2. Loïc Wacquant, "Scrutinizing the Street: Poverty, Morality, and the Pitfalls of Urban Ethnography," *American Journal of Sociology* 107 (May 2002), 1501.

3. Elijah Anderson, *Code of the Street: Decency, Violence, and the Moral Life of the Inner City* (New York: W. W. Norton, 1999).

4. Sudhir Alladi Venkatesh, *Off the Books: The Underground Economy of the Urban Poor* (Cambridge, MA: Harvard University Press, 2006).

5. Deirdre Bloome, "The Interplay of Structure and Culture in Perpetuating Black Urban Poverty" (unpublished manuscript, Harvard University, May 2008).

6. Patrick Sharkey, "The Intergenerational Transmission of Context," *American Journal of Sociology* 113 (2008), 931–69; and Robert J. Sampson, Patrick Sharkey, and Stephen W. Raudenbush, "Durable Effects of Concentrated Disadvantage on Verbal Ability among African-American Children," *Proceedings of the National Academy of Sciences of the United States of America* 105 (2008), 845–52.

7. I thank Eva Rosen for this insight (private communication, July 4, 2008).

8. Bloome, "Interplay of Structure and Culture."

9. Richard J. Herrnstein and Charles Murray, *The Bell Curve: Intelligence and Class in American Life* (New York: Free Press, 1994).

10. Other social scientists have reached similar conclusions in their critique of *The Bell Curve*. For a discussion of these reactions, see Orlando Patterson, "Taking Culture Seriously: A Framework and an Afro-American Illustration," in *Culture Matters: How Values Shape Human Progress*, eds. Lawrence E. Harrison and Samuel P. Huntington (New York: Basic Books, 2000), 202–18.

11. Ulf Hannerz, *Soulside: Inquiries into Ghetto Culture and Community* (New York: Columbia University Press, 1969).

12. Robert Asen, private communication, May 7, 2008. Readers interested in Asen's work should consult his book *Visions of Poverty: Welfare Policy and the Political Imagination* (Lansing: Michigan State University Press, 2002).

13. Lawrence Bobo, "Race, Interests, and Beliefs about Affirmative Action," *American Behavioral Scientist* 41 (1998), 986.

14. Lawrence Bobo and Ryan A. Smith, "Antipoverty Politics, Affirmative Action, and Racial Attitudes," in *Confronting Poverty: Prescriptions for Change*, eds. Sheldon H. Danziger, Gary D. Sandefur, and Daniel H. Weinberg (Cambridge, MA: Harvard University Press, 1994), 365–95.

15. Barry Bluestone and Mary Huff Stevenson, *Greater Boston in Transition: Race and Ethnicity in a Renaissance Region* (New York: Sage Foundation, 1999).

16. Lawrence Bobo and James R. Kluegel, "Opposition to Race Targeting: Self-Interest, Stratification Ideology, or Racial Attitudes?" *American Sociological Review* 58 (1993), 446.

17. Comments by Ronald Haskins at a conference titled "The Moynihan Report Revisited: Lessons and Reflections after Four Decades," Harvard University, Cambridge, MA, September 27, 2007. I used the words "in the years immediately following passage of the 1996 welfare reform bill" deliberately. With the subsequent drain on the budget caused by Bush's regressive tax policy, the Iraq war, the war in Afghanistan, and the fight against terrorism, all of these programs have suffered deep cuts.

18. Wilson, *Truly Disadvantaged*; and Wilson, *When Work Disappears*.

19. "Transcript: Senator Barack Obama's Speech on Race" (March 18, 2008), at www .npr.org/templates/story/story.php?storyId=88478467.

20. Wilson, *Truly Disadvantaged*.

21. See Leon Litwack's amazing history of Jim Crow: *Trouble in Mind: Black Southerners in the Age of Jim Crow* (New York: Knopf, 1998).

22. Patterson, "Taking Culture Seriously."

23. Sharkey, "Intergenerational Transmission of Context"; and Sampson et al., "Durable Effects of Concentrated Disadvantage."

24. Sandra Susan Smith, *Lone Pursuit: Distrust and Defensive Individualism among the Black Poor* (New York: Sage Foundation, 2007).

25. Ibid., 37.

26. Kathryn Edin and Maria Kefalas, *Promises I Can Keep: Why Poor Women Put Motherhood before Marriage* (Berkeley: University of California Press, 2005).

27. Bloome, *Interplay of Structure and Culture*.

28. Lawrence Bobo, James R. Kluegel, and Ryan A. Smith, "Laissez Faire Racism: The Crystallization of a Kinder, Gentler, Anti-Black Ideology," in *Racial Attitudes in the 1990s*, eds. Steven A. Tuch and Jack K. Martin (Westport, CT: Praeger, 1997), 15–44.

29. Bruce Western, *Punishment and Inequality in America* (New York: Sage Foundation, 2006).

INDEX